GIFTS

Remembering the NOW

Yolanda Zigarmi Martin

OUGHTEN HOUSE PUBLICATIONS
LIVERMORE, CALIFORNIA, USA

Gifts: Remembering the Now
by
Yolanda Zigarmi Martin

Copyright © 1997 by Yolanda Zigarmi Martin
Published 1997

00 99 98 97   0 9 8 7 6 5 4 3 2 1

Published by:
OUGHTEN HOUSE PUBLICATIONS
PO BOX 2008,
LIVERMORE, CALIFORNIA 94551-2008
PHONE: (510) 447-2332
FAX: (510) 447-2376
E-MAIL: oughtenhouse.com
INTERNET: www.oughtenhouse.com

Library of Congress Cataloging-in-Publication Data
Martin, Yolanda Zigarmi   1942
    Gifts: remembering the now / by Yolanda Zigarmi Martin
      p.   cm.
    ISBN 1-880666-59-6 (pbk.)
    1. Martin, Yolanda Zigarmi, 1942-   2. Reincarnation -
- Biography. I. Title
    BL520. M37A3   1997
    133.9 '01' 35--dc21
                                     97-2058
                                     CIP

ISBN 1-880666-59-6, Trade Paperback
Printed in United States of America

TABLE OF CONTENTS

DEDICATION

This work is dedicated to my spiritual teachers, those invisible Beings who offer you, as well as me, their limitless patience, unconditional caring, and continuous guidance. It is because of their presence and love in my life that this material can be presented.

In Gratitude

This book is a tapestry woven of many threads. I thank all the unnamed people and circumstances whose influence is entwined in these pages.

I am grateful to my husband for his great capacity to love and allow me my journey, for his support, and his loving arms, and my step-daughter, Christina, for her radiant essence, and her ability to give and receive love.

I honor my family and ancestors for their gifts of spirit and transformation: my father, for the many roles he played; my mother, for always seeing the God in me, even at the cost of human hopes and dreams; my brother, for providing me with an ideal. If I can love all life as purely as I love him, then I shall see God in all things.

I am grateful to Billy and Lorraine Sayer for volunteering to be with me in this life experience and sharing the joy of the work.

I thank and honor all the special friends and healers who have graced my life, filling it with laughter, tears, and ever-expanding love: Muriel Lindsay, Edward Lambton, Elli Ennis, Ann Mills, LeRoy Zemke, Mavis Mobley, Julia B. Davidson, Jay Youngblood, John Doriss, Stephanie Blackton, Elizabeth Muirhead, Peter Scuphan, and Joseph Mina. So glad you all are here.

I honor Oughten House for their commitment to Light and Love, and Robert Gerard for his vision and courage. My gratitude to Tony Stubbs for his care in editing *Gifts* and for his enormous inner strength and sensitivity, which eases my heart.

I honor you, the reader, for you are the Light of the world.

LETTER TO THE READER

If you are at all like me, you will want to skip this letter and get on with the "real" reading, but please do take a moment to read these few pages, as it will establish in your mind the purpose behind this book.

I am by nature a very private person, so while the telling of this adventure in spiritual awareness is exciting, it is also uncomfortable for me. I write it in the hope that it may be valuable to you. It is because of the underlying truth in this spiritual journey that I expose my deepest thoughts and experiences. It is not because I wish you to think I am special in any way. I am an average person living an ordinary existence. You and I could easily meet in a check-out line at the grocery store and exchange pleasantries.

My life is probably not much different from your own. What you are about to read is the journey of a regular person into the inner realm of spirit. I can take you to the door with me and let you look into a universe of soul, but if you wish to enter this infinite world of wonder and beauty, *you* must find your own key and open your own door. Hopefully, reading this book will remind you where you left your key and that your door is closer to you than your next breath.

Before starting, let me tell you of the how and the why of this book. It began with a phone call from my very close friend, Lorraine Sayer. We have known each other for many years, and I shared with her some of the experiences and the revelations I had received. Lorraine had just finished reading *Embraced by the Light* by Betty J. Eadie. She wanted me to read it because the experiences Ms. Eadie had when she was clinically dead were much like some of those I had related. Yet, I had not died.

I did read the book and I saw in it confirmation of all I had learned in my inner search. But instead of feeling uplifted and validated, I felt terribly frustrated. From that frustration, and from the support and encouragement of Lorraine, this book was born.

In the past few years, a myriad of books relating personal "life-after-death" experiences have been published, opening the minds of many people. I am thankful for and recognize the courage required by those who have written of their after-death experiences. However, the majority of these books tend to leave the reader thinking that such experiences are available only to those who die. One objective of my book is to show that such knowledge can be acquired during this life and without a death experience. So although I have not died, I have had experiences which confirm that Life is a continuing journey into ever-expanding awareness, with its beginning in Infinity and therefore having no end.

Most religions teach that life is eternal, and many of us accept that. But do we really believe it? Do you believe it? Have you considered what eternal life means to you, personally? Those who have had a "life-after-death" experience *know* eternal life is a reality. I, too, have accessed eternity and *know* that life is eternal through my own personal experiences. It is my wish that this book may bridge the gap between hoping that life is eternal and *knowing* it is.

Although these events are my personal experiences, I hope that as you read them they trigger an awareness of your own spiritual identity. These events changed my life drastically, always for the better. Perhaps they can change yours. Of course, the words and the narrative in and of themselves have no power to change anything, but the underlying spiritual Truth can, if accepted, awaken memories within your own soul.

What is this underlying spiritual Truth? That there is a part of you that is All-Knowing, All-Present and All-Love, Infinite and Eternal. Therefore, the simple truth offered here will continue to expand and deepen as you allow your own beliefs and concepts to stretch.

I firmly believe that given a choice between ignorance or truth, most of us would choose truth. If you are reading this book, you are at least open to considering that there is more to life than our physical senses tell us. My sincere request is that while you read this book, you do not judge it or me but rather take into your heart what is true for you and simply discard the rest. What you recognize as Truth, whether it be my experience or your own, will act as a catalyst in your individual spiritual journey; the rest may be a catalyst for someone else.

Another important thing I have learned on this journey is that you may throw Truth away a hundred times, a million times even, but if you desire to know, it will keep coming back to you and presenting itself until you recognize It.

So please relax and read on. You may consider this a novel, an autobiography, or science fiction. Consider it anything that will allow you to read it. The Truth is not in the teller but in the Truth itself. Think of this book as a gentle reminder of what you have always known in your own heart.

PREFACE

It was difficult to put into words the essence and meaning of the experiences you are about to read. Language seemed more of a hindrance than a help. Since the choice was either using inadequate words or writing no book at all, I opted for the words and trust that the spirit behind the words will convey their meaning and purpose. I have used capitalized words when referring to the portions of ourselves that are God aspects. For example, in the word self, Self is our spiritual nature, and self is our personal human nature; Consciousness is our God-awareness, and consciousness is our personal self-awareness.

The book relates, in chronological order, several spiritual experiences and their gifts, how they effected my day-to-day existence, why they were revealed at a particular time in my life, and what accumulative effect they had on my awareness of self and God.

You will find that the narrative becomes more complex with each successive experience. This is because each experience expanded my awareness of the eternal Self. For this reason, I have divided the book into four sections. Section I reads like stories from the pages of history. Section II, although not difficult to read, may require you to stretch. The comfortable historical settings of the past, seen in Section I, are altered, and the actual information shared lies outside mainstream thinking. Section III is dedicated to questions and answers. Most of these questions were generated by students and friends of mine. Some questions I posed myself, because I felt that to address them in the text would detract from the reading. And finally, the Epilogue ties it all together in a surprising gift of insight.

It is my hope you will read the entire book, but you may want to take a break between sections. The intention of this chronicle is to activate the memories which we all have of our true spiritual nature. Awakening spiritual consciousness is like an unlimited feast of possibilities, and like a banquet, in order to sample everything, you may wish to savor, rest, and digest slowly. I encourage you to pause when you find you are trying to dissect and intellectually understand the content. Relax, since this book is meant to provoke *your* knowing and not necessarily for you to understand *my* knowing. Feel free to skip to the question/answer section if a pressing question should arise. Often, we ask the same questions, and you may find a freedom in just seeing the question asked.

Please keep in mind that the answers to these questions are *my* perceptions, coming to me from *my* experiences. We may all ask the same questions, but because each of us is our own Truth, each of us has his or her own answers. Trust yourself.

SECTION 1

As I cried, I prayed to my invisible teacher, "Help me, please help me." I felt her smiling as she whispered, "Help yourself. Simply step forth and be the Divine Being that you are."

Even as she spoke I felt a great calm. I saw how all the past experiences had allowed me to come to this moment. I was grateful.

Being given this loving admonition, I decided after much soul-searching to "surrender" a part of myself and take you with me on a spiritual journey which is continuing to unfold even as you read.

Chapter 1

THE BEGINNING

"Please, please let me do this. Please let me go in." I am in a huge light-filled hall. Although there are no visible doors or walls, there is a sense of containment. I am surrounded by a beautiful, deep bluish-purple color, a color unlike any I have ever seen. Although the color is dark and rich, it is also luminous, full of light. My plea is directed to a tribunal of three huge Beings of Light. I am aware that their power is enormous, yet totally benign. The entire space is filled with a great peace, joy, and love.

I am conscious of Myself. I feel radiantly happy, child-like in my assurance of Self and the love of all those present. I am the same being that I am now, only somehow more complete. There are no words spoken, only imprints of communications being transferred, but in blocks of information rather than language.

I know as I face these Beings of Light that they represent a vast Spiritual Hierarchy. They are exalted, omniscient, loving Beings. As I beg to be allowed to fulfill my request, I am conscious that there is absolutely no judgment from the tribunal, only a moment's hesitation. In that flash of hesitancy, I can feel my deeply profound yearning for this opportunity. I am quite clear that if not allowed this chance, I will not feel hurt or even disappointed. It is only that I have a great love to do this work, and it is love that I wish to express in this commission.

As the tribunal hesitates, I become aware of two Light Beings, one on either side of me. I can feel my connection to them and the mutual love that we share. They are offering to be part of my experience. They promise they will be with me. With their commitment, the Hierarchy agrees at once. I am in ecstasy. I am ready.

I remember being born. It was an experience of being squashed, then suddenly cold, and then an unsettling, actually horrifying, sensation of feeling very foreign. It has taken most of my life to lose that feeling of being a stranger in an even stranger

3

land. For years as a child I would ask my mother if I was adopted, never feeling quite at home or familiar in this life.

Not only do I remember my birth but also being in my mother's womb. I have only a vague sense of a body and seem to have been mostly a thinking, feeling creature. I believe one reason I remember this state is due to the impact of having to make the decision as to whether I would go ahead with my birth or turn back.

I do not know how long I had been attached to this embryonic form, but at some point I became conscious that there was a physical form and I was connected to it. I was feeling happy and taking much comfort in the rhythmic swishing, thumping sounds around me, when suddenly I felt something coming into me, being fed into me, of which I had no control. It was at that moment that I realized I had been, for lack of a better word, "pure," but now something not of that purity was being forced into me. I remember thinking, "I can refuse this, this energy. I do not want it. It is not mine or me." But I was aware that if I did refuse, I would not be able to enter into this human experience; the embryo I was attached to would be aborted. It was quite literally a do-or-die situation, and obviously I chose to accept that energy and go through with the birth.

So, what was that all about? What "energy" was I forced to accept? I believe it was the realization of the genetic encoding of the family into which I was being born, plus the awareness of whatever emotional, physical, and mental events my mother was experiencing. I say this because the memory and conscious awareness of that embryonic self was the same awareness of self that I now have. The major difference between that remembered self and the present me is that up until I decided to accept the energy and be born, I was conscious of a purity, an innocence, and an uncontaminated state of being, all of which changed the moment I accepted the genetic encoding and, of course, with the birth itself.

As for the actual birth, I remember being aware of how much more difficult it was than I had envisioned. If you do not remember your own birth, you might well ask how I could have anticipated what being born would be like. The answer is simply that before you are born, you are Life; after you are born, you are that same Life. And after you die? You are still that same Life.

You and I as infants may have arrived in a package that looks and behaves in an immature and undeveloped fashion, but that is not the reality; it is only the appearance. By the time we have gone through the trauma of birth, our memory of pre-existence grows dim. When I speak of birthing as traumatic, I am not so much referring to the physical demands made upon a newborn. The more lasting trauma is the sudden shock of having to go from limitlessness and clarity into constriction and limitation. Our Being is immediately restricted, not only in form (physical body) but also in movement, since babies are completely dependent upon adults for their worldly existence and mobility. Our Being must now rely on a structure (body) that isn't even working at full potential and will not be for at least a decade and a half.

Take a moment and imagine that you are an ocean (Spirit Being) with all its variety, energy, and freedom. To enter a human body, you must take what you can garner from your own vastness and scale it down to fit into a tiny bottle. For that reason birth is traumatic, and after such a shock, many of us forget our true roots and our real identity. Yes, forget, but only forget. We do not lose or forfeit but simply experience temporary amnesia.

The antidote for this state of forgetfulness is to stimulate ourselves to remember, to find the key that will unlock that memory. Expanding our awareness or consciousness beyond our physical senses opens the doors of memories and experiences and the door to our Divine Being.

Coming home from the hospital as a newborn and being put on the chenille bedspread in my parents' room is still a clear picture in my mind. Clearer still is the feeling of panic that went through me. I was certain I was in the wrong place. I had not seen anyone I expected to meet. It was like making future travel plans with friends: you each agree to travel to a designated place at a specified time, each from a different direction. You understand you will be alone in your journey until you meet at the appointed place. You arrive, but they are not there. I, the self that I am today, was in that new-born body. I was a fully conscious being, capable of thought and of memory, but in a little baby body.

I recall lying on my parents' bed as the feeling of panic increased with each moment. I wanted to scream, "Help! Get me out of here," when suddenly my father came into my line of vision. He smiled down at me and I recognized him at once. A wave of relief passed over me as I thought, "Oh, I know you. You're familiar," and some of the hysteria abated. Shortly thereafter, my brother came over to me. To my immense relief and joy I knew him and thought, "Okay, this is the right place." I then settled into being in a physical body, never quite comfortable and always feeling a little alien.

Years later I told these memories to my mother. I described the furniture and its placement in the room, the chenille bedspread, the sequence in which I saw my father and brother. She was astounded by the detail and correctness of my memory, and told me she had developed a severe cold soon after I was born. For that reason she had kept her distance when I first arrived home.

I have had many memories which reach even further back in time. Often they are accompanied with teachings and lessons. The memories arise spontaneously during waking hours, usually while doing such mundane things as ironing and cleaning house. What I have come to realize is that these are not fictional stories but are memories of experiences of my own Divine Being and expressions of Infinite Consciousness.

Do not let the word consciousness distract or confuse you. It is simply *all* that you are aware or conscious of. You may be aware of many things on many levels at the same time. For example, you may be aware of a headache while feeling anxious about not having heard from your daughter who was due home over an hour ago. At the same time, you are balancing your checkbook. All of this is happening simultaneously.

As you think of your daughter and say silently to yourself, "Oh, I hope she's all right," you suddenly feel intuitively that she is fine. In that moment, you are operating on four different levels of consciousness or awareness at the same time: physical (the headache), emotional (your anxiety about your daughter), mental (as you worked on your checkbook), and intuitive (as you inwardly "knew" that your daughter was safe). We take this multilevel awareness for granted because we are accustomed to it and because such manifold awareness is shared by most people.

Many of you have experienced your sense of intuition and not thought it strange or incomprehensible. Why couldn't that same multiplicity of consciousness or awareness extend deeper, even beyond intuition, into areas that have been touched by people who have experienced life after death? Doesn't it seem reasonable that if such areas exist for them, they exist for us all?

For some unexplained reason, I have been able since birth to tap into those areas of what I call Expanded Consciousness. I have often been aware of more than is evident through just the physical senses. I believe this is due in part to the retentive power of my memory. But we all have the memory of our birth recorded in our subconscious, available to us if we wish to search it out. Once we remember being born, why would it be such a great step to remember the time before birth?

My early years provided an environment for me, even as a very young child, to reach beyond my physical limits. Although I grew up with a devoted mother and a loving brother, the first decade and a half held much turmoil and distress for us as a family. Those early years were filled with verbal and physical abuse between my parents. My father's quick and unpredictable temper frequently overshadowed his many talents and brilliant intellect. During this time, I was often comforted and supported by what I thought of as my "fairy person." This was a Being that appeared to me as a white flying horse, a Pegasus creature.

As I learned later, the ever-available help of our spiritual family comes to us in a form and a way that we can understand and accept. Some other child might have perceived such a Being in the guise of an angel, but with my intense love of animals, a flying horse suited my nature. He would hover by my left ear on my shoulder and speak softly to me, always lovingly and with great patience. I say "speak," but actually they weren't words but blocks of complete ideas that I would then mentally put into words if I felt the need. Mostly, I didn't need words because the transmitted block was sufficient. If I had to "speak" to him, I would start a thought but before I could finish, he would have answered. Communication between us was rapid and without the clumsiness of language. Sometimes I would see him when other people were around and sometimes when I was alone.

The older I grew, the more he would instruct me in the quiet and privacy of my room. He would never tell me when it was time for a "lesson." I would simply pick myself up and go off to my room and then the instruction would begin. Years later, both my mom and brother admitted that my abrupt withdrawals would perplex them. Fortunately for me, both loved me and trusted my judgment enough to allow me those quiet times.

My invisible teacher's instruction was always given in "language" that I could understand. As I grew older, his "language" and lessons expanded. The most powerful lessons he taught me had to do with letting go and being detached. As a child, it would have been easy to internalize the turbulence between my parents and make their distress my own. Here is where my invisible teacher was ever vigilant, constantly whispering to me to turn my attention inward, that within my heart is a quiet place, a place of perfection. He reminded me over and over, "Your parents' experience is their experience, not yours. You have your own work. If you try to enter into their experience, you will miss your own. It is for your own journey that you are here." Even though I was a very young child (two and a half onward), I understood perfectly what was being said to me.

He would caution me not to confuse the *person* with the behavior they were displaying and stressed how important it was to love the *person*. Although it was easy for me to love each parent, regardless of their behavior, I did not understand until many years later that true loving brings about true forgiving and that true forgiveness is absolute freedom. Only now do I recognize that this is one of the most important lessons that we as human beings can learn.

From this invisible Being, I began to appreciate and incorporate into my character the qualities of silence and of seeking my own inner counsel and place of balance. I learned the value of detachment, not just from things but from ideas, beliefs, people, and expectations. Once having instilled these lessons within me, my teacher gradually disappeared from my life. By the time I was a teenager, I seldom saw him or heard from him. During those years, I did remember that I had a teacher, but the actual teachings themselves were forgotten for the time being. Neither my teacher nor his lessons seemed important to me then. Like most teenagers, I was too busy with my social life, studies, and working after school. I no longer felt that I needed him. However, to my immense joy and total surprise, he was to return in a form and in a way suited to my adult life.

Even though I had this spiritual support as a child, it did not keep me from accumulating emotional baggage, but it did help me move through it with great speed and some degree of grace. I am grateful for the special people in my life who shared techniques and knowledge that allowed me to dump so much of the emotional energy I accepted in ignorance.

Have you ever considered how much emotional debris you have accepted as "yours" that really has nothing to do with you?

Chapter 2

THE PREPARATION

Although my outer life took a normal path for the most part, the one major recurring theme from my teen years to mid-thirties was a kind of longing, a deep desire, a restlessness for an unknown something that would bring me contentment. Like most people, I thought if I could acquire more things, make more money, and find the perfect relationship such restlessness would cease. And again, like most people who have acquired outer satisfaction, I was still left feeling discontent. From all outward appearances, I should have been more than satisfied with my life, but I never was.

I attended four years of college, taught public school for three years, and left teaching to return to graduate school. Graduate school led me into the business world, which in turn took me to Atlanta as general manager of a company opening a new branch office in the South. Being in Atlanta was significant, for at that time it was alive with metaphysical study centers and a thriving esoteric community.

Within two years of my move to the city, the company I had been working for was sold and I was without a job. At first there was an urgency to find another management position as I went through all the ordinary channels and interviews. When nothing seemed to be exactly right, I decided to take a year off, use up my savings if need be, and stop running wildly about looking for the perfect position.

It was at this juncture, due to a passing comment by a friend, that I began to explore the realm of metaphysics, and what began as a casual remark was, in fact, the first step of a boundless journey of soul.

I entered into the study of metaphysics partly skeptical but mostly curious. My curiosity evolved into the earnest seeking of spiritual wisdom and I soon found myself on a path of self-disciplined study.

In retrospect, losing my job was actually a gift of spirit and not the disaster I had first perceived. It is strange how often our soul's desire makes itself known through crisis. Without having been pushed out of the business world, I am sure I would never have explored this inner world.

What I remember most about this new exploration was both its newness and at the same time its familiarity. My fondest memory of this period was reading for the first time, *The Kybalion,*[1] a treatise on the Seven Principles of Hermes Trismegistus. As I read, my heart pounded with excitement, for with the turn of each page I knew exactly what was coming next. I remember thinking to myself, "I know this, I already know this." Waves and waves of information would flood into my memory.

I wish there was some way I could convey to you the wonder and the thrill of those moments. In this lifetime, I had never heard of Hermes Trismegistus. In fact, I could not even pronounce the name, never mind know the subject matter. Yet I found myself not only knowing in detail each Hermetic law but *understanding* easily and clearly the principles presented. And this knowing came as though I was simply reviewing material I had learned in the past. In fact, it was more like remembering.

So it was with almost every other author of esoteric literature I read for the next few years. I had never been exposed to these authors and their philosophies, yet they were as old friends, and the content, a comfortable perusal. I was happy, contented, and feeling for the first time that I was in the right place and doing the right thing.

I was unemployed and I would read sixteen to eighteen hours a day, hating to stop even to eat. Gone was the restlessness and

[1] *The Kybalion*, Three Initiates, The Yogi Publication Society, Masonic Temple, Chicago, Ill, 1940

discontent, and even the sense of feeling alien abated. It was a most joyful time. Along with the wonder of unfolding information, came a period of being exceptionally psychic. Yet even the psychic aspect of my life paled next to this burning need to reacquaint myself with as much information as I could.

As a result of this rapid unfolding, I was soon teaching classes at various metaphysical institutions on meditation, reincarnation, karma, esoteric psychology, and color awareness.

Teaching was exciting and rewarding for it gave me a chance to refine and practice what I felt I already knew. This was a period filled with many friends and social activity. In time, I was not only teaching but counseling as well. The opportunity for one-on-one work was beneficial for both parties and stimulated each of us to seek clarity and apply the principles. I can see how important this work was, for it helped cement into my conscious remembrance all that was needed in order to understand what was yet to come.

My days were filled with studying, teaching, remembering, exploring Western and Eastern philosophy, and deepening my ability to meditate. It was a time of cultivating discipline, and instilling dedication and a desire for more and more Truth. Eventually I stopped teaching and counseling and turned my attention from metaphysics toward more mystical teachings.

The experiences and information that make up this book are expressions of Consciousness or Being revealing Itself. It is the same Consciousness we all have, in varying degrees of individual awareness. The awakening of this inner Consciousness was incited and nurtured by those years of study, meditation, and dedication. This Consciousness is like a lake that has been dammed up for years. At first it is very difficult to make an opening in the dam. With effort, you can begin to see a drop ease through, then two drops, and gradually the water begins to drip and then trickle, growing to become a stream, and then a river flowing into an infinite ocean of Awareness.

I was once again to meet the invisible teacher of my child-hood. I had been out of town for Thanksgiving to visit my brother and his family. My mother was there, along with relatives of my sister-in-law. It was a warm family occasion but I was impatient with myself. I could not seem to stick to my routine of medita-tion early in the morning and in the evening. I found it hard to settle down and get quiet enough to meditate, and always there was something else I could or wanted to do. By the time I re-turned to my apartment in Atlanta, I felt disappointed in myself, thinking that perhaps I should not have taken time out from my study, even for a holiday. I judged myself lacking in discipline and dedication—a verdict that generated acute frustration. After unpacking, I fell into bed and slipped immediately off to sleep.

I woke about 2:30 a.m. to find myself sitting up in bed, and my physical body still lying prone, as if I had two bodies. The one I was conscious of being in was much lighter than the one lying in bed. I had the sensation of being in the physical body from the waist down and in this lighter body from the waist up, kind of half in and half out of my physical body.

At the foot of my bed was a tall slender figure. I remember sensing clearly that it was masculine, but in appearance it had no gender nor did I see a face, only a tall, soft blue form. I thought that I should be frightened but wasn't. It seemed normal to me and I was feeling quite contented. Whoever or whatever this was, on some level of my awareness it appeared routine. I smiled, lay back into my physical body, and promptly returned to sleep.

The next morning as I recalled the experience I was perplexed and awed but still did not feel there was anything amiss with such a visitation. I did notice that the frustration and self-berat-ing of the night before had gone and I could reflect on the time I'd spent over Thanksgiving without feeling disappointed in myself.

Soon after, on various occasions during meditation, I would see a beautiful indigo color before my eyes and feel a warmth fall over me. For months that color and feeling were all I was aware of, and it was always the same. Occasionally a statement from Scripture or something inspiring would drop into my awareness. At first I thought it was just my subconscious remembering pieces I had read. In retrospect, it seems odd to me that I did not recognize the difference between being taught and my own thoughts. As a child, it was always so clear when I was receiving a lesson. Now as an adult, it never entered my mind.

One afternoon I was at a metaphysical center talking with a friend about reading material. He suddenly stopped talking and asked me, "Who is that man?" I had no idea who he was talking about; I couldn't see anyone. My friend then began to describe a person who he apparently could see clearly but I could not see at all. Before my friend could finish his description, I was certain he was describing my Thanksgiving night visitor. Then almost simultaneously I realized this was not only the Being I had seen at the foot of my bed Thanksgiving weekend, but my wonderful friend and teacher from childhood. This was my "fairy person" as he is, not as he presented himself to me as a child. I felt such joy and excitement.

Once I recognized him, I could ask for his presence and guidance. He would come, as he had always come to me those past few months, as a warm feeling and the color indigo. I love him and am ever grateful for his help and guidance. I continually learn from him and seek his guidance, especially when worldly clutter and activity cloud my spiritual vision. He was with me through my childhood and then through the years of metaphysical study and teaching, guiding and offering me an unconditional love rarely experienced in human relationships.

The relationship between us and our spiritual guides is not limited to only a few "sensitive" people. It is a divine gift—no, it is our divine right—as we seek to know our true identity, as we seek to know our God. Such a sacred search is fraught with doubts and seeming difficulties, especially in the beginning. Our teachers are ever-present and available to offer clarity and comfort. They desire nothing more than for us to ask for their friendship and guidance. This you can do the same way you would address any person. You need only ask sincerely that your spiritual teachers make themselves known to you. It is their joy and privilege to be a conscious part of your life.

When and how they reveal themselves depends on your receptivity and accessibility; that is, how open you are to receiving help. Are you making time in your busy schedule to listen?

At first it may require a bit of faith or inner trust on your part. And do not get discouraged if nothing happens after asking once or twice for your guides or teachers to make themselves known. They know you very well, better in fact than you know yourself, so they are not likely to present themselves to you on a whim or just to satisfy your curiosity. After you ask for their presence, be open for any sign. It may be a particular color in meditation, as with me, or a feeling, or a scent in the air. It could even be through a series of coincidences that they first begin to interact with you. If you ask they will answer, so you must be alert to recognize their presence. Then after a while you will find how best to communicate.

When you are ready and sincere, when you truly ask, they will answer. It is important when they do, that you acknowledge their presence and give thanks for their help. Doing so strengthens the bond between you. I am very grateful for my spiritual family and for all the blessings their relationship imparts. Such support was necessary to prepare me for what lay ahead.

Chapter 3

THE FRENCH WOMAN

Several years passed during which time my studies became more inner-directed. Up until then I had been gathering information, remembering, and studying. I made a conscious commitment to myself to live a life (as much as possible) that was true and spiritual in action, not just in words. It is easy to learn the jargon and spend a lifetime collecting the right words of any particular study, be it spiritual or scientific. The hard part is living it, integrating it into daily habits. Spirit recognizes when we make a deep, committed decision to live life from the highest level of our understanding of Truth and does everything to support our commitment. It's like putting our spiritual money where our mouth is and then reaping immediate rewards from a universe just waiting to rain its treasures over and through us.

Soon after making this commitment, the universal rains came! What marvelous rains they were, too, for they were about to wash away and transform layer upon layer of misconception.

It was a normal sunny afternoon. I was ironing, facing the window, and looking out at the beautiful clear day, not thinking of anything in particular, just mindlessly waving the iron across a stack of blouses. Suddenly, I felt an intense sorrow, an emotional pain very deep inside of me. I had no idea that such intensity of feeling was possible until that moment. It was so extreme that I felt physically sick in my stomach and in my heart. Simultaneously, a mental image of a ceramic heart shattering into a million pieces shot through my mind as I thought, "My heart is breaking, literally it is breaking and crumbling."

Even as I felt the pain, I was sure the source was not my physical body. Although this was a peculiar perception, I wasn't frightened. Moving quickly, I turned off the iron and sat in the

chair I usually meditate in. I was barely seated before tears fell—
no, they gushed in torrents—as if gallons of tears had been stored
up behind my eyes and all at once every one wanted out. I didn't
know why. My heart pounded with excitement and curiosity, while
at the same time I felt it breaking with sorrow. I closed my eyes
and through the tears I became aware of a "movie screen" behind
my eyelids. It felt like my eyes were open and I was watching a
movie, except it was three-dimensional. I was looking down on a
scene, as if from a balcony, yet I could see as if I were looking
straight ahead as well. It was a most fascinating experience for I
was simultaneously the observer, the action, and the arena where
the action was occurring. It was an odd kind of *déjà vu*, like having been here before, part of this same action before, and now I
am participating in a kind of rerun.

*I am looking down into a wide entrance way with stone floors,
dark carpets on the floor, and tapestries on the wall. It is France,
sometime in the mid-16th century. Light streams in from a hidden
source. At the end of the hallway are tall wood and metal double
doors next to a stone staircase. Three girls are gathered in a circle.
The two younger girls of about seven and eight are laughing and
tugging at the older girl's arm. They are playful with her and she
smiles at them tolerantly. The older girl appears only about thirteen
or so, but in attitude and demeanor she seems closer to thirty. I sense
their warmth and humor as they huddle and whisper together.*

*In a room off the hallway which would have been called a li-
brary if there were more books, an older man pours over rolled maps
and documents. The girls in the hallway are sisters and the man in
the library is their father.*

As I view the scene, all knowing is impressed upon me in an
instant, like a photograph; snap, and a fraction of a second cap-
tures thousands of points of detail, history, and feelings.

The oldest of the three girls is "me," but at another time and
place in Consciousness. As I watch, she becomes a young woman
of about eighteen. She is very lovely to look at, a beautiful intel-

ligent face, erect figure, and long graceful hands. I know her. I recognize her. I am her. I know this is my experience in another lifetime. This recognition evokes waves of love for the young woman and for the experience.

Knowing without a shadow of a doubt that she is somehow a part of me is hard to explain, but it is similar to seeing someone in a dream who doesn't resemble you at all, but you know it is you.

This young woman is the eldest daughter of a wealthy, accomplished, and landed family. She has strong opinions, and is encouraged by her father to develop her intellect and scholarly inclinations. She is intelligent, artistic, fiercely independent, and loves learning. Along with these qualities, she has developed the traits of superiority, pride, vanity, and an unforgiving nature. She evaluates people and judges them by the harsh standards with which she judges herself.

Being the eldest daughter, she must marry before her younger sisters can but she will accept a man only of her own choosing. Her family, lands, and income make her more than desirable but since her character is very serious and precise, such a process proves to be long and arduous. This is due to her perfectionist nature rather than a lack of admirers.

Finally, after many an interview, a suitable man presents himself. Almost instantly, she projects her ideals and needs onto this man, seeing him as she would like him to be, which is not really who he is. Once married she surrenders her whole identity to him—body, mind, and soul. They move into a large and lavish estate given to her as a wedding gift from her father. Within a few months she allows a young male cousin to come and live with her and her husband. The cousin wishes to study with her, to learn geography, languages, and music. This pleases the young woman for she enjoys displaying her intellect and indulging her love of learning. At first it is a satisfying arrangement. She is happy. She has an adoring student who worships her talents and knowledge. Her husband is pleased for entirely different reasons.

*The marriage proves to be a disaster. Her husband's sexual incli-
nations are not toward women nor does he try to hide his predilec-
tion. He flaunts his sexual preference before her, in her own house,
by carrying on a liaison with her young male cousin. Her pride and
passionate spirit are shattered. She abdicates her strong indepen-
dence, stifles her pride and, in short, loses her identity. All this is
done in an attempt to make her husband love and need her as she
needs him.*

*She begins to feel that her husband wooed, married, and de-
ceived her for her land, money, and position but acknowledging this
is extremely difficult for her. She had always seen herself as being
the pride and prize of society and was certain she would be desired
for her wit, intellect, physical beauty, and grace.*

*Recognizing her error makes remaining in the marriage unthink-
able. It is absolutely impossible for a person of her uncompromising
standards to live a lie of such magnitude. In a state of emotional
devastation and despair, she and her maid-companion leave the
house. She flees to an old castle keep on the coast of France which is
a part of her dowry lands. Here the young woman lives out the remainder of her life, alone and in seclusion except for her maid. She
refuses to see members of her family or anyone from society as her
humiliation is brutal. She is totally damaged emotionally and feels
she has no identity. She feels powerless and without defenses .*

*In time, a friend of her father comes to offer solace and intellec-
tual exchange. The self-imposed isolation is harsh, broken only by
the tutelage and friendship of her father's elderly friend. He is an
unusual scholar. Her father has sent him to comfort her and, more
importantly, to persuade her to return home.*

*The old scholar is not a traditional teacher but a man who prac-
tices the ancient sciences and is sometimes referred to as a magician.
It isn't magic at all but simply understanding and using universal
laws. I recognize the magician instantly as my father in my present
life. He does not look at all like my father, but I know without hesitation it is him. With this recognition, I feel overwhelming love and
appreciation for my father, and for all he has taught me both then
and now. It is a gifted moment.*

*The magician tries to coax the young woman to return to her
father's house. He struggles to lift her spirits and convince her that*

all will be well if she would just return home but she will not even consider such an option. She feels the humiliation of her failed marriage is hard enough to endure alone; it would be impossible to bear in the presence of her father, mother, and sisters.

Although she refuses her father's plea to come home, she consents to the old scholar remaining as her teacher. He introduces her to the Ancient Wisdom, esoteric teachings, and information he has mastered from various secret societies. He instructs her in the use of energy, how to manipulate it, how to quiet and control the mind, and how to read the stars.

The old scholar comes to her rooms two or three times each day. In the beginning, he comes mainly to comfort and to persuade her to forgive and go home. This, of course, is impossible for her. She is too proud, too hurt, too unforgiving of herself. She forbids the magician to speak to her of her family. He may only instruct her. She is, however, a diligent and able student and finds consolation in the daily lessons. She applies her strong will and ardent intellect to all his teachings. He is delighted to have such a capable, serious student, not to mention a captive audience.

As the years pass, the old magician begins to feel that his young student is softening, that her pain is easing. He hopes that in the near future he will be able to induce her to return home and resume a normal life.

As I watch, I am acutely aware of her emotional pain and her intense character. The years of exile have served only to increase and strengthen her emotional scarring. I want to step into the picture, to take her hands in mine and comfort her but, of course, I can only watch.

Imagine the helplessness of seeing someone and knowing exactly how they feel, knowing they need to be comforted, knowing they feel that no one can possibly understand their hurt. But you do understand, without judgment, yet you cannot reach them. Even if you could, they would not accept you. My sorrow is now doubled, for I can feel hers and now my own.

The old magician has misjudged his pupil and her motivations. One quiet autumn day, she knows she has learned all that is required. She has learned well and feels confident once again.

It is late afternoon. She enters a small room on the uppermost floor of the castle. She has been coming to this room many, many times, unknown to her teacher or her maid. There is a small narrow slit window on the rounded side of the outer wall. Weak sunlight filters through this slit, making a pattern on the stone floor as the cool air wafts gently through.

Opposite the window is a cot with a throw and a small pillow, both beautifully embroidered. She has made these pieces herself with this particular afternoon in mind.

She enters and closes the wooden door with deliberation. With great intent, she latches the door and walks to the cot, her body straight and determined. Her bearing displays the qualities of control and confidence she possessed before her marriage. With the reverence of performing a ritual, she lies down on the cot and painstakingly arranges her dress. She places the embroidered throw over her body from the waist down to her feet. She lies on her back, adjusts the pillow beneath her head, and places her arms straight beside her. She closes her eyes for just a few seconds, then opens them, looking up at the ceiling.

It is a strange moment. I am looking down on her, lying on her back and she is looking up, staring with her eyes wide open. Of course, she cannot see me but it feels as though she should be able to.

*She does not move except to breathe. She doesn't even blink her eyes; they remain open. Her chest moves up and down with one last prolonged breath. Her eyes remain open until she detaches her consciousness from her body, **willing it so**, and at that moment, her eyes flutter shut.*

I am aware that I have almost stopped breathing myself as I watch this scene. Everything is still—the air in the room where I am, the air in the room where she is. My breathing has slowed. My breath is silent.

I watch, acutely attentive, scarcely breathing as she literally lies down and wills herself to die. I am mesmerized as much by the scene as by the implications of what I see. I am aware of her and her feelings as I watch her now-lifeless body. She had felt such profound hurt, had been so distraught and despairing when she had lain down.

As I watch, I become less of an observer and more the participant. I begin to feel her absolute despair, her intensity, her complete resignation. I feel the fullness of her will.

At the moment her Consciousness disconnects from her body, I experience her overwhelming sense of awe, joy, and freedom. I feel her recognition and realization that Consciousness is what we are, that the physical, mental, and emotional experiences we have *are not us*. At *her* moment of understanding, I feel her and the entire experience become me. I feel myself whirling with an inner joy and freedom of completeness yet unknown to me. Up until that moment, there had been an odd kind of oneness in which I was her, yet I was observing her. Self watching self. A "me" watching and a "her" doing and being. But at *her* moment of understanding, we become one and the same Being. I am her and she is me.

I am clearly aware that this is a past life of mine, of me as I am now. No past—just now and only NOW.

I remained quiet and still for a long while, feeling such immense gratitude for this experience that tears of joy and appreciation streamed down my face.

Chapter 4

GIFTS FROM THE FRENCH WOMAN

After the experience of the French Woman, I didn't know what to do. A part of me wanted to call everyone I cared about to share this experience, while another part wanted to hold it close, to protect it and keep it secret. There was yet another part that was asking, "What was that? Was I dreaming? Is my blood sugar low? Did I have enough protein this morning?"

I had decided early in my metaphysical life that I would consider every "experience" and every "enlightened person" suspect. If the experience or person was true, it would prove itself. That was the attitude I took toward this experience, more out of discipline than desire. From my heart and from that elusive place called my Soul, I knew this was a real and gifted experience. Yet I was determined to give my mind the opportunity to prove me wrong.

So I had a past-life revelation. It was interesting, exciting, heart-wrenching, and at the same time fun. Now what? File it away in my journal as a bit of phenomena?

The feelings around this experience were mostly those of awe and appreciation, with a strong sense of gratitude for having been shown this memory. As I reconciled myself to this having been a past-life memory, I felt my first consideration had to be to question why. Why this particular past life? What was there about the French Woman of the 16th century that was relevant to a young woman of the 20th century?

So I began a kind of serendipitous pondering. At first it was a casual wondering, not too deep and not too often. It was not until pivotal changes in my own being became gradually apparent that I gave this experience a more serious examination. It was, and has been, easy to recall the episode in detail because it was indelibly imprinted in my memory.

When my consciousness merged into the French Woman's as she detached herself from her body, her entire feeling nature became available to me. I knew at that moment what she felt and thought. Her emotional experience was etched in my heart, from actual vision to unknown facts and particulars.

Here was a young woman with a strong intellect. Her father had brought her up as he would have a son, encouraging her to expand her knowledge in all areas. She was allowed a great latitude of expression and was able to explore areas of learning that were, at that time, reserved for male scholarship. Her father involved her in finance, science, and mathematics. As a result, she was steeped in pride of intellect and self-importance. She became the center of her own and her father's world socially, emotionally, and intellectually.

Her life consisted of her father, her erudition, occasionally her sisters, and somewhere in the faint recesses of her mind, her mother. That there was little emotional connection with her mother was interesting. It was apparent that until she married, her loves were knowledge and the learning shared with her father.

I sense that if she had been allowed to live a single life, with just learning, discussion, and debate filling her days, she could have had a very satisfying life. Such was not to be her fate. Her confidence in her innate intelligence and her arrogance in her desirability as a wife gave her little opportunity to develop discernment in relationships. This was partly because of her scholarly nature and partly because she always felt superior to both the men and the women around her. She considered only scholars worthy of her time and effort.

Once she determined that she was to marry, she set about the task with precision and calculation. As suitors presented themselves, she would measure them, critique them, test them even, only to find each one wanting; no one could measure up. Her sisters, being centered in domestic and artistic affairs and disinterested in scholarship and mental acuity, urged her to be less meticulous. When at last, under constant pressure from her sisters, a man meeting most of her exacting criterion offered marriage, she accepted.

It was apparent to me that in her marriage she was entirely self-directed; that is, her thoughts and feelings centered exclusively on her personal reflections, judgments, and opinions. She gave no consideration and little thought to her husband or how he interacted with her. Everything was measured through "I, me, mine"—"How *I* feel…how much *I* love…how *I* hurt…*my* heart breaking…*my* pride damaged…how could this happen to *me*?"

I was never conscious of her husband beyond the fact that she saw him as having been responsible for her misery. I have tried to imagine what this "perfect" man must have been like and the qualities he must have possessed to have deceived her so completely. I imagine that he was quite bright and that he recognized her enormous pride of intellect and egocentricity. Such qualities could make one easy prey for a charming and resourceful man of opportunity. But here I must reserve judgment, since the expectations for a married couple in the 16th century would be vastly different from the expectations of a 20th century couple.

It seems reasonable that her husband was simply what he had presented himself to be; possibly witty, definitely bright, and undoubtedly desiring a suitable situation to increase his wealth and property. I had to ask myself if it could have been her unrealistic expectations and lack of discernment that lead to such a drastic conclusion to her marriage.

Granted, from her perspective, her husband was indiscreet regarding his sexual preference and most likely did not relish the physical obligation of marriage. Yet the purpose of a 16th-century marriage was as much, if not more, for alliance, material gain, and security. Factors such as love and personal commitment were less important. Did she create in her mind an unrealistic alliance, an imaginary union where she would be the center of her husband's universe in, and on, all levels? They must have been equally clever, sharing in the pleasures of learning and she must have found his company entertaining or she never would have married him. Could she not have compromised and avoided such drastic measures? Probably not; she was unyielding and unforgiving and this left no room for negotiation, no space for compromise.

As for the total surrender of herself to this man, I can only rely on what I have seen in this lifetime regarding bright, independent, self-confident women. Somewhere, somehow, there seems to be a place within some women—and actually not just in women but men as well—that feels incomplete. For instance, a particular person would enter into their life and elicit a sense of completeness, of well-being. This feeling might conjure up such a powerful sense of wholeness that they could be tricked into believing that they are not whole to begin with and could only experience wholeness by surrendering themselves to another person. Of course, such surrender can be dangerous and is built upon an erroneous premise.

The reality is, you are in and of yourself *whole* already and cannot be made any more complete by another person or any other external addition. This is a fact which I have always been keenly aware of in this lifetime. I think I learned it from this French Woman's experience. You see, this quality of wholeness and self-completeness had been deeply ingrained in me, branded into the very fabric of my being for as long as I can remember.

I can understand how she must have felt as she began to realize that her expectations for marriage were not going to be fulfilled. Surely she felt incredulous and confused that she was no longer the center of the universe as she had always been. Bit by bit she began to give up parts of herself, to change her behavior, and to become a stranger to her previous self. She did this in order to make her situation conform to her expectations. Such an endeavor was doomed to failure. Yet hasn't each of us done the same thing at various times in our lives?

Over a relatively short period of time, she had gradually forsaken her true identity for this man and the marriage, leaving her vulnerable and devastated. That, coupled with her total unwillingness to be forgiving, especially toward herself, made the remainder of her life a prison. Her self-imposed isolation sent her deeper into a state of severe self-judgment and self-criticism. Although this happened four hundred years ago, such behavior may be seen in many modern relationships.

As I watched her lie on the cot before detaching herself from her body, it was clear there was no remorse or forgiveness in her heart. She was hardened in her pain and personal disappointment in herself. She was sorry, yes, but only because she had allowed herself to be deceived into a disastrous marriage. Even after years of exile, she lay on the cot still incredulous that she, of all women, could have made such a grave error.

Until I had this experience I was often inwardly and, occasionally, outwardly critical and intolerant of others, especially when it came to my women friends. I would watch their behavior in and out of relationships and think to myself, "How foolish they are. Why do they give up parts of themselves for someone less worthy?" As it turned out, my friends were, for the most part, having a good time experimenting, in fact, learning what was and was not important to them in relationships. Fortunately there were no seriously broken hearts in my circle of friends—a few cracks and an occasional chip—but nothing irreparable.

The criticism and judgments that I held in my mind and heart, however, were not conducive to living what I considered to be a spiritual life. With the experience of the French Woman, those critical, judgmental feelings gradually dissipated. I found, somewhat to my surprise, that I had become more tolerant without actually being aware it was happening.

As time passed, I felt myself getting lighter, as if I'd been carrying some invisible weight around on my shoulders and it was lifting. I was happier and less zealous about achieving my goals of swift enlightenment and instantaneous illumination. I relaxed into this French Woman's experience, not questioning or really even looking too deeply to see if my life was changing. But my life *was* changing.

I had married when I was in college and found the state of matrimony not to my liking. This was no reflection on the man I married, for he was a loyal, true, and good person. It was simply me. I felt confined, unable to be myself (whatever that meant; I didn't know, but it was how I felt). I didn't like the commitment of marriage, so I divorced.

The years following my divorce were filled with romances but not commitments. Obviously I was not willing to make a personal commitment to a relationship. I was engaged several times to men who were bright, capable, and loving, the type of men most women would find little serious fault with. Most of my friends couldn't understand why I didn't make it to the altar. In fact, neither could I but in looking back on these relationships, I always had an excellent excuse for not marrying: I felt I was too intelligent for them. In time I knew I would get bored and I really wanted someone who was intellectually superior to me. I, too, felt like this French Woman! Really, there were no grounds for this intellectual snobbery on my part; although I went to graduate school and was in a Ph.D. program, I never wrote the dissertation or received my doctorate, yet I had this sense of intellectual superiority.

Now I could begin to understand where this feeling came from. I had these feelings of superiority down to my core. It was not just in my mind; it came from somewhere deeper and permeated my total self. The odd thing about this intellectual elitism was that I didn't warrant it in terms of college degrees or even in outward attitude. Also, I never considered myself an intellectual, even though many of my friends thought me so and classified me as cerebral, which always amazed me. I did have many acquaintances who were scholarly and bookish, but frankly, I found them a bit colorless; I much preferred puttering in the kitchen to doing the *New York Times* crossword in ink.

Thanks to the experience of the French Woman, I was beginning to understand so much that was, until now, a puzzle. How grateful I was for this awakening.

Gradually, the information gleaned through that past-life experience was integrated and accepted into my being. The many subtle and obvious alterations in my character revealed themselves in the form of a new life and identity. I was able to make a lasting, loving, and trusting commitment. I have been married now for well over a decade and have no doubt that the revelation of this experience with the insight and healing it brought to me is what made it possible. Ironically, my husband is a gifted, brilliant engineer and not in the least boring.

In the years that followed the French Woman memory, I became more consciously aware of how hard and exacting I was on myself and on others. The French Woman taught me how, taken to extremes, such qualities as self-criticism and perfectionism can destroy rather than develop one's character. Both characteristics are valuable as we try to stretch to our highest potential, but they are simply tools. They are not the goal. Her intensity of purpose was so overpowering that it obscured her discernment. If she had chosen to turn that intensity towards developing a forgiving nature or towards compromise, her life could have had a totally different ending. This experience has taught me the importance of forgiveness and its power of restoration and regeneration, and to cultivate a less meticulous lifestyle, to relax the severe inner standards I have set for myself, and to simply lighten up.

I have often wondered if those souls who were so much a part of that experience in France in the 16th century have touched my life now. Certainly my father in this present life was the magician in that past life. My father was actually a very powerful man who could manipulate people and situations with his mind and his intense presence. In intellect and in talent, he was very much a Renaissance man. Although he never ascribed to the doctrine of reincarnation, he was aware of a deep recognition between us. We had a strong, loving bond from the moment we greeted each other the day I arrived home from the hospital.

There is something else about my father in this lifetime and as the 16th-century magician. I can see, thanks to that French memory, how much my father had chosen to forget when he came into this lifetime. For him or for any of us to have a particular life experience, we must be selective as to what knowledge we will bring into conscious remembrance. I could see how selective he had been. He did not remember what he had taught me in that 16th-century life. I know that when I began to study metaphysics, the simultaneous reading and remembering primarily involved the information that the magician had taught the French Woman while she was in exile. However, my father did not seem to remember that his power came from understanding and using the same universal laws that the magician had mastered. All that information would have been available to my father in this life if he had turned his energies toward a path of conscious spiritual searching. That he did not is not important nor of consequence, only of interest.

I have recognized only one other person from that experience who is here in my life today. I feel blessed that we are able to experience another time and another place together.

My mind now agrees with my heart and soul that I had indeed had a real healing experience. I believe this experience was given to me because through daily choices and dedication, I had made evident to my soul that spiritual growth was my goal. I realized this knowledge had been imparted to me because there were some qualities of the French Woman I had carried over into this life that were hindering further development of soul. Even today, I am aware that I still must work on aspects of intensity, self-criticism, and judgment. If these qualities had remained hidden, they would have created confusion and doubt in my search for a deeper understanding of Spirit. By remembering that lifetime, by examining it, and by embracing it as my own, a healing took place in my consciousness. And as with all spiritual healing, it was really a *revealing* of some aspect of Being. This experience has changed my life forever.

I have come to realize that when such an experience has permanent repercussions in your life, when it alters forever the way you act and react to your environment and the people in it, then it is more than just an experience; it is a change in Consciousness. Dreams, fantasies, and imagination are useful as psychological tools, but they do not usually create permanent changes in consciousness or awareness. This I believe is because they are only tools and not truths. Truth revealed can and does bring about permanent change in consciousness. I use the word consciousness often in this book and define it as *what you are conscious of, what you are aware of.* The more Truth you are conscious of, the more you become *what is true* rather than what you *believe to be true.* And what is this truth? Simply put, it is that we are Spirit Being appearing as human being in physical/material form. That form is only our *appearance*; it is not our *Self.*

The French Woman experience allowed me to participate *consciously* in the realization of spiritual Consciousness. When the French Woman detached herself from her body and became aware that, even without a physical body, *she was still an individual being,* I experienced that awareness and her sheer ecstasy of BEING. I know these are just words and as such are inadequate but if you can catch even a fleeting glimpse of such a state, then you may recognize your own true nature. It's the difference between being a man, a woman, or a child with needs, likes, dislikes, and worldly judgments, and just being an unencumbered BEING.

This experience was a personal one, meant for me and about me. Its purpose was to restore to conscious memory the energy of the original root experiences that were interfering with the progress of my soul. Once I understood these experiences, they were unified into a more perfect concept of Self. I believe that when we are born into a lifetime, we are looking to reunite aspects of self with Self (Divine Being or Soul). When this unity takes place, we experience healing,

How do we know when a life issue has been healed? It is healed when it is no longer an issue, when it has been ingested into our being. It is then neither a good issue nor a bad issue. Where there was a problem, a concern, or a conflict, there is now only a sense of completeness or wholeness.

The experience of the French Women was the only one I had of that nature for some years. But coming to terms with it triggered something of a metamorphosis in my life. In the coming years, I was to have other spontaneous memories: I would close my eyes and allow my eyelids to be the movie screen. It seemed that my eyes were open and I was both the audience watching the action and in the action itself. Not only did I see images but also received smells and sounds. Sometimes I would just observe, but other times I would connect with the people in the scenes, feeling their emotions and hearing their thoughts. Also the perspective of the screen could change; I could be in front of it or above it looking down. I experienced a strange duality of being both separate and connected. I was the privileged outside observer and at the same time I was part of the action, especially at the moment of union between me in my present life and the characters in their present lives.

Chapter 5

THE MONASTERY CHILD

Years had passed, during which time I had married and settled into a comfortable life. The next episode began during a routine morning: coffee, reading the newspaper, and kissing my husband good-bye as he left for work. Once alone, I usually began the day with some spiritual reading, a meditation, and then on to the tasks of the day. I was making the bed when I felt a strong urge to return to meditation.

I went to my chair and closed my eyes in order to become quiet and silent. At once I heard sobbing, deep, deep sobbing, loud and all around me, similar to being in a noisy restaurant where the din seems to permeate every corner. This resounding weeping over, under, and beside me wasn't confined to my internal senses but also assailed me externally. Engrossed in listening, I didn't have a clue as to what was happening. As I grew accustomed to the sound, a picture formed on the inner screen behind my eyes, exactly as it had years before with the French Woman experience.

A diminutive girl, a child actually, is curled up on a stone floor, her head buried in her arms. The room looks like a cell, but in a monastery rather than a prison. It is built of large blocks of grayish-brown stone that radiate the cold. There is nothing friendly or inviting about it. The cell is austere, with no furniture visible. On one side of the cell floor is a bed of straw with a ragged blanket folded neatly on top. The child is not lying on the straw, but is huddled on the damp stone floor. No light is apparent in the cell, yet the girl is easily visible. Her frail, little body is undernourished and shivering with the cold. It is the Middle Ages.

The child wears a dark tattered tunic, greatly worn and patched, that almost totally hides her body, with just her small head and dark hair visible. She is not wearing shoes. Her feet peer out from under her robe; they are small and dirty. The sight of those tiny feet makes her seem abjectly pitiful and helpless.

The stone floor under her is icy cold. Gradually the temperature of the cell registers on my body. I begin to feel how cold she is, and then her thoughts enter my mind. She is not speaking aloud. The only sound coming from her is a bottomless, grievous whimper escaping through her tears and wrenching sobs. She is thinking, "I have sinned against God. I have left God out of my life. I shall never be forgiven." Her crying is unconstrained and her fragile little body quakes under the coarse fabric of her robe.

I am acutely conscious of her feeling of eternal damnation. This terror is a most peculiar sensation, one I have no frame of reference for, either in my mind or emotions but I feel it completely.

"I have trespassed against God," she repeats in horror at the kind of after-death she imagines to be in store for her. She believes she will languish forever, suffering horribly in some hideous existence, unable to reach God in order to ask for forgiveness. Her desire for forgiveness is second only to her intense love of God. She truly feels God no longer loves her, and this is more unbearable than any punishment she could ever imagine. It is beyond hopelessness!

I have no idea what her transgression is. Whatever her offense might have been, it is dwarfed by the imagined punishment of the loss of God's love. I am aware of her misery, her emotional despair, her sense of doom. As I sense all this, I am also aware that I am the observer, and in this impersonal perception, I feel strongly that whatever she believes she has done is not as grave as her imagining. Somehow I am certain that what she is judging her sin to be would not be considered so drastic a transgression today. The centuries separating her from me have so altered moral and ethical criteria that I know without a doubt that her self-torment would be amiss today. With that thought, the experience ended abruptly.

I had observed this picture without personal emotion. I didn't feel especially involved with the Child, other than receiving her thoughts and feelings telepathically, yet oddly when it ended, I found myself shaken and unable to stop crying. Uncontrollable sobbing welled up from some unknown place within me. I had no clue as to why, nor from where these feelings came. The Child did elicit sympathy and compassion, but certainly what I felt was much more than commiseration. Not only was I crying, but my heart and mind were consumed by a tremendous restlessness.

Several hours had passed and I was still distressed. I could not analyze or process this experience because I could not quiet my mind or emotions long enough to think. This was a new and disturbing development, for discipline of mind had never been a problem for me. I decided to call a psychologist friend who had counseled people through past-life memories. Her assurance was soothing and insightful.

First, she did not think I was crazy or in the throes of a mental breakdown. This was comforting. Second, she advised me to try and "contact" the girl in meditation. My friend suggested that if I could communicate with the Child, I could comfort her by showing her that I was *her* future. In so doing, I could demonstrate to her that she would not be doomed but would evolve into the being I am today. This advice felt exactly right.

Over the next few days, the emotion and restlessness became less invasive. During that time, I tried in meditation to contact the Child on several occasions, but to no avail. Thinking there was nothing more I could do, I recorded the experience in my journal and let the memory rest as simply a record of a time past.

Several days elapsed during which I spent many hours reading, meditating, and in quiet contemplation. Then while going about my ordinary household chores, the Child spontaneously appeared to me without warning but in a manner quite different than before. The picture of the Child did not play itself on my inner screen. In fact, I had no indication she was about to appear. I didn't have time to sit down or close my eyes. One moment I was walking across the bedroom, and the next I was looking at the Child curled up on the cell floor. Space and time suddenly had a large doorway in it and I could see clearly into the Child's cell of the 1300s. The abrupt appearance of the Child in this manner didn't seem unusual to me. I only cared that I could see her again.

As she appears directly in front of me lying on the stone floor and sobbing, I feel a quiet appreciation for this opportunity. I speak to her through thought. I silently ask her to look up. She doesn't seem to "hear" me at first. I plead with her, "Please, please look up," which she does after several moments. She lifts her head from her arms and turns toward me. Huge, naive and sorrowful eyes set in a gaunt, petite face look up at me. She looks about ten or eleven years old and very fragile. As she gazes up, her hands and wrists become visible. They are tiny and unwashed.

She looks up toward me, but I do not know if she can see me. I think she senses me more than sees me. At first I think the words to her, "You are forgiven," several times. I wait to see if she reacts, but she still doesn't seem to hear me. I urgently want her to receive this message so I speak aloud to her, "You are forgiven...it is all right...see...I am here. Look, I am you and you have become me. You are forgiven." Still curled up on the stone floor, she looks toward me for a long time. I don't hear her think or say anything, nor does her facial expression change in recognition of my communication. The doorway then collapses and disappears.

I am aware in that moment that I was not so much an observer as a messenger. I didn't identify personally with her nor did I have a reaction after this second encounter. I simply sent a message, letting her know everything was all right. I felt I had done all I could, and that would probably be the last I would see of her. I had no particular thoughts or feelings about this episode; it seemed strangely normal and yet filled with wonder.

I thought after this contact with the Child that I would not see her again; that was not the case. Days later she appeared once more, but this time more like the first episode. I was working around the house when the impulse intruded to stop and sit quietly. Obeying this inner urge, I sat down, closed my eyes, and a picture unfolded.

The Child walks along a covered stone walkway outside a massive building constructed of the same stone. The outer wall of the building makes up one side of the walkway; the other side has huge stone openings exposed to the weather and to a courtyard. She is wearing a long, dark, rough fabric robe with her head covered. Her feet are bare except for a pair of sandals. It is wintertime; light powdery snow blows onto the pathway.

She follows behind eight or ten other women, all dressed alike and walking in pairs. The other women have passed my field of vision so I cannot see their faces or sense how old they are. Each seems to be engrossed in her own thoughts; no one notices when the Child lags behind.

She will die of sickness soon and she is aware of this. She feels calm and serene. She walks in front of my "screen." She stops ... she turns ... and looks directly INTO me. We are eye-to-eye, her eyes wide, sad, resolute, and without expression. There is no animation in her face. Without moving, she stares at and into me for a long time as the other women walk on. Then, with deliberation, as if in slow motion, she turns away and disappears.

When this experience ended, there was no residual reaction or feeling; it just seemed complete. When the child looked directly into my eyes and we held each other's gaze for several moments, it was both startling and somehow incredibly right. It didn't seem unusual. She didn't seem foreign to me, nor did I feel any particular emotion. It was a moment frozen in time, a moment of pure timelessness. I was now certain this experience had completed itself. There was a sense of finality to it. I had no idea that there would be still another chapter in this story; another truly gifted moment with this Child yet to come.

Chapter 6

THE MONASTERY CHILD CONSIDERED

My first response to this experience was to relegate it to the realm of past-life memory. This felt right, mainly because of the intrusions of the previous months. For many days prior to this experience, a passionate need for forgiveness infiltrated my meditations and contemplative reading, accompanied by a compelling sense of repentance.

Although I was brought up in the Catholic Church, orthodox religious training and devotion fell away once I reached my teens. In fact, aside from *The Lord's Prayer* and *Now I Lay Me Down to Sleep*, I cannot remember a single prayer of the church so moments of penitence felt peculiar. Stranger, too, were the several episodes during meditation where I would find myself beating on my chest, reciting *mea culpa, mea culpa* and searching for the words of the Act of Contrition.

The need for absolution was always accompanied with an inexplicable feeling of spiritual unworthiness. Of course, it is not unusual for people on a spiritual path to feel unworthy: brushes with Divinity can serve to magnify our humanness. Such a sense of unworthiness I was familiar with, but this felt different. It was more of a medieval religious feeling. Naturally when the Child in the monastery began appearing to me, I assumed she was the source of those unexplained religious feelings—an old memory coming forward to be recognized and united. This was confirmed when the feelings disappeared after my encounter with the Child.

Happily I accepted the experience as further evidence and as reinforcement of the continuity of identity, or the ongoing nature of the soul. Still, I was bewildered. In many ways, my emotional response to the first encounter with the Child was complex and penetrating. It had considerably more emotional impact on me than did my first experience of the French Woman. The feelings and emotions in the first observation of the Child remained alive within me for many days and are still with me today.

Try as I may, I could not find the link between the Child in the 1300's and me in this lifetime. The French Woman experience was clear, for she and I shared similar characteristics. We felt and thought in similar ways. The purpose of the memory was easy to grasp, once I began examining it. However, the Child in the monastery was different because of our dissimilarity. Had it not been for the intensity of the emotion that this experience generated, I would have recorded it simply as a past life and forgotten it.

In retrospect, I can see how important emotions are in these experiences. First, they allow a cathartic cleansing to take place, a purging of what no longer serves us, thus making way for new insights. They also act as attention-grabbers. Emotions can function the same way in dreams. An otherwise unremarkable dream might be remembered solely for its emotional impact. We are apt to give both dreams and regression experiences greater consideration and permission to express themselves because they jarred us on a deeper level. If the actual experience doesn't seem to reveal its message to us at once, at least the emotional response will keep us alert until something else emerges as an explanation.

It would be many months before the far-reaching significance of the experience with the Child would be revealed. Looking back, it seems strange that I would have thought the sole purpose of this experience was to recall a past life. It was curious, too, that I seemed only to consider the first encounter as important and hardly thought about the space-time doorway episode or even her departure as we held each other eye-to-eye. For months I questioned why the Monastery Child lifetime presented itself at this point in my spiritual journey. Each time I came to the same conclusion: It didn't seem significant except for the intensity of feeling it generated. It seemed to be "for information only."

It was not until much later that the significance of the Child in the monastery would become apparent, and at that time she would tell me in her own words.

Chapter 7

THE CRUSADER

Time passed and life progressed as usual, yet weeks before this next experience took place, a thought would intrude into my meditation: "I wish I could get out of here!" I knew that "here" was my physical body. The intense feeling of being entombed or trapped inside the body produced a peculiar sense of duality. There was a perception of a "me" and a body separate and apart from me. We did not function in a symbiotic relationship but rather as prisoner (me) and prison (body).

Also I occasionally had the peculiar feeling that some heavy weight was resting on my chest, so with each breath I would feel my chest pushing against some invisible object. I felt that if I could just use my fingers to somehow open my chest, I could slip out of the body and leave this heavy feeling behind. At this point in my life, I had come to recognize the difference between "an experience" and my present existence, so I knew without question that I was not having medical problems. The physical sensation was both real and separate from me. I knew these occurrences were clues in a puzzle that would reveal their purpose in due course. I needed only to wait.

One morning I was speaking to a friend on the telephone about the place and function of memories in our lives. As we talked, tears filled my eyes and that odd, heavy feeling reoccurred. By the time I hung up the phone, the pressure on my chest was so strong that I had difficulty breathing. It felt very real and very physical.

I sat down, closed my eyes, and spoke silently to the unknown memory causing this feeling, "Okay, I acknowledge you, I welcome you." I tried to take deep breaths and not succumb to the sobbing. Instantly my screen showed a picture. This was a differ-

43

ent kind of experience. I was conscious of a physical and emotional event, but there was also a smell, at first faint and unidentifiable. The chest pressure intensified. I felt trapped in my body and wanted to peel if off. I thought, "If only I could cut open my chest and part my ribs, I could slip out and be free." I was aware of both watching and feeling the pictures on my inner screen and at the same time being the person on the screen. I sat there with my fingers curled, knuckle to knuckle on my breastbone, digging into my chest. My ribs throbbed as my fingernails dug into my skin.

Suddenly there he was, the focus switching from me personally to him. My fingers relax and my hands press to my heart. Feelings of love and great tenderness for this person fill me. I recognize him as someone very dear and a sense of tranquillity settles on me. All that he is is impressed upon me in an instant— his feelings, emotions, loves, and his fears.

He looks so small, almost a miniature figure lying there. He is well past middle age, intelligent and someone who has had more than his fair share of life. He does not want to go to war. He has no strong feeling for any religious doctrine. A poet and a scholar, he believes all should be free to live as they choose. Yet he finds himself in a Holy War, fighting, killing, and hating it all.

Now he lies under a lone tree in a hot, barren, landscape. The sun is setting...again. He has been in this place and this position for many days. A smell fills my nostrils, a nauseating, rotting, putrid smell. Something crawls on my left arm and right leg. I reach down to brush whatever it is away but I realize nothing is crawling on me. They are crawling on him—flies, insects, and maggots squirming and eating the flesh in the wounds of his arms and legs.

He is encased in a suit of armor. His chest is twisted, the bones pushing on the unyielding metal. He cannot move his head in any direction; his helmet grips his head like a vice, the result of a fall. He cannot even shake off the flies. He can barely moisten his lips with his tongue. He lies rotting in his armor. His immense pain is apparent, yet I feel only the crawling sensation of the insects, the weight of the armor, and the smell of the sickening stench. I am both horrified and curiously detached.

He thinks, "I must get out" (meaning from the armor). Oddly enough, he is quiet and calm and seems oblivious to the maggots and the smell of rotting flesh. His sole intent is to extricate himself from the armor. He repeats over and over, like a mantra, "I must get out."

The sun rises and sets, and it takes him many days to die; he simply rots to death.

Suddenly his spirit is free from that body and the excruciating experience. At once I am him—floating, whirling, released. The Earth spins and the armor lying on the ground below grows smaller and smaller as I rise. I feel incredible bliss and joy. I hear him say laughingly in a young man's voice, a beautiful voice, "That was great! When may I do that again?"

His words shocked me. Instead of savoring the ecstasy of the moment, I literally snapped out of the experience. The feelings of joy and bliss remained with me and gradually turned to gratitude, but I didn't understand what he said or how he felt. I knew I felt his appreciation for the life he had just completed, and even for what I perceived as a horrible death. It took me several hours before I could begin to process this experience, but I knew it was a full and an important gift.

Chapter 8

GIFTS FROM THE CRUSADER

U ntil this experience, I did not consider a lifetime a privilege; it had always seemed to be more of a penalty. I secretly agreed with a friend who joked that Earth is the penal colony of the universe and that each of us is here serving time in varying degrees of discomfort and brutality for our past transgressions.

Also, ever since studying and accepting the concept of reincarnation, I had *never* wanted to incarnate again. I could not imagine choosing or even desiring to voluntarily return for another round of human experience. It may sound as though I went through life in a state of depressed discontent, but that was not so. Laughter, friendship, and discovery were as much a part of my life as my dedication to spiritual ideals. It was simply that human life didn't seem to make much sense. I felt that what we accept as human existence is not really life. It seemed to me this life was a kind of marking time until the *real life* presented itself. The *real life*, I felt, was what we experienced after we mastered the "unreal" human one. It was life lived without fear or judgment. Consequently, I was not keen on having to return for more unreal life if I had a choice.

This attitude became a standing source of amusement with friends, most of whom enjoyed their human journey. When reincarnation would come up in conversation, they would voice preference for talents and dispositions they wished to explore in their next incarnation. I, on the other hand, would have to be tied, gagged, and forcibly thrown into a human body. This, of course, was said in jest, yet the underlying reality for me was that I did not relish the thought of another experience in human form.

Can you imagine how astonished I was at that moment when I became one with the Crusader and felt his appreciation for, and sense of enjoyment of human existence? It was so different from what I would have expected.

There was no question in my heart and mind that the Crusader was and is a part of my own ongoing soul experience. I knew I was him and he was me in that instant when he left his earthly body. As the person I was when that memory occurred, I know I would have said something more along the lines of, "Please don't make me do it again," rather than, "When may I do it again?" Clearly this experience would take work to understand and integrate.

Now I had to rethink what I held to be true regarding reincarnation and its purpose. I had come to believe a generally accepted premise regarding reincarnation: That we set particular circumstances in motion through our emotional attachments or, more specifically, through our ignorance of spiritual Truth. We are responsible for what we set in motion. "As ye sow, so shall ye reap." Consequently, whatever wrongful thing we set in motion, we must at some point have the opportunity to set it right, and we have as many opportunities to correct mistakes as necessary. We must learn thoroughly what, why, and how our mistakes came about. The same goes for any good or rightful thing we may have accomplished; we are given opportunities to receive these rewards, recognition, or benefits.

I understood reincarnation in terms of spiritual evolution in that as we refine our conduct through understanding spiritual Truth, we became less attached, more tolerant, and eventually enlightened. The culmination of this evolution would result in a state of permanent illumination or Oneness with God (the Infinite Invisible or whatever your concept of that which is All-Knowing, All-Present, All-Powerful, and All-Loving. The word God works for me.)

I imagined this spiritual evolution as a giant cone-shaped spiral leading from our earthly existence up into Oneness, the bottom ring of the spiral being the widest and each successive ring growing narrower and narrower. Eventually, the spiral becomes a single point or finally the place of Oneness. This was a very finite view of an infinite concept, but it was an understandable and comfortable one for me.

Such a view had allowed me to take responsibility for all of my actions and reactions in this life. I felt we could, at certain stages in the spiral, make a leap to the next level without having to complete an entire ring. That leap would be made possible by living according to our highest spiritual ideals. Although the spiral allowed for jumps in consciousness, it was still a movement from lower awareness to higher, in steps and in time.

How did the lifetime of the Crusader change all this? With his desire for another experience, a new and even more startling insight dawned in me.

I knew the Crusader to be a highly-evolved soul. He was conscious of a life that reached far beyond his physical awareness. He had moments of enlightenment. He understood a deep, profound truth about the soul's journey toward union with the God-Self. He did not hold a single trace of malice, anger, or resentment for his plight or death. Although I was, as the observer of this moment, acutely aware of his bodily pain and the sensations regarding his long, drawn-out death, *he was not.*

The thought of the French Woman and how she desired to leave her body and her life experience replayed itself. Her only motivation was to free herself from her intense emotional distress. Her penetrating self-judgment and lack of forgiveness of herself and others were still very apparent in her consciousness when she died. She was relieved when she freed herself from her body, that the experience was over. That she recognized she was not her experience but that she was Consciousness was both enlightening and profound, but it pales next to the awareness of the Crusader.

The Crusader had no concern or attachment to his dying condition. He had transcended physical pain and was so immersed in the reality that Consciousness is what we are, that his physical situation ceased to intrude upon his awareness. When I heard him thinking, "I must get out of here," he was speaking of freeing his *consciousness* from the body. Because I was reacting to his physical predicament, I had thought he meant freeing his body from the armor. But he had gone beyond his physical condition and was centering his attention on his spiritual Self.

When I understood that I was conscious only of his physical plight yet he had dismissed it, an extraordinary insight struck me: He was fully aware that this particular lifetime was ending and that now it was time for a new experience. He was actually in a hurry to brush off the dust of this experience, not to escape pain and suffering but simply to begin a new challenge. The circumstances of his dying were irrelevant to him. In fact, he considered the lifetime he had just completed, in and of itself, largely irrelevant. It was the opportunities human existence afforded him that were relevant, not the actual day-to-day existence.

And then it struck me: There is no time, at least not time the way we think of time. There cannot be. The Crusader's lifetime took place in the 11th century, and he was an extremely conscious being. Granted, he was not living in a permanent state of enlightenment, but he was having glimpses of that high state of Conscious Oneness and incorporating those glimpses into his life's experience. Next came the Child in the monastery, somewhere in the 14th century. She seemed far, far from the enlightened awareness of the Crusader, believing in hell and eternal damnation. Now I could see the reason for the memory of the Child in the monastery. Her importance, I felt at that moment, was not so much the lifetime, but the time of the life. It was a link in the chronological order of these past lives. She gave credence to there being no time as we perceive it. Next came the French Woman in the 16th century, also not as conscious as the Crusader. And then there's me in the 20th century, struggling to achieve a glimmer of God-Consciousness.

The wonder of it! The Crusader is an aspect of my soul and he, in the 11th century, already had a greater, a more expanded awareness and sense of the Truth and the Reality of Being than I.

Of course, such a revelation sent me reeling. Oddly, within a day or two, all of this information seemed to settle into a divine harmony like a mystical kaleidoscope in which each new design forms a higher, more refined and accurate picture of spiritual reality. When you look at the design, it seems perfect. You turn the wheel and watch as all the pieces shift and scatter and for a while there is no beauty or design, just chaos. Then the pieces begin to fall into place and a whole new, beautiful picture emerges more refined and perfect than the previous one. You have not added new pieces or changed the frame in which they move; you have simply raised the way of looking at the same elements to a more exalted perspective. This was how I saw the Crusader's experience functioning in my consciousness.

The Crusader considered life a privilege granted to the soul. Life was not a punishment or reward for past deeds or misdeeds but an adventure, an opportunity to express the boundless qualities of individual spirit. For a moment I could almost grasp it. I could see that, as Infinite Beings, we desire to express our infinity in a myriad of ways, one of which is human consciousness. In the human experience, there is resistance and pairs of opposites. These two conditions allow us to make choices. By making choices, we exercise and develop our spiritual awareness to the point of Oneness. Here, in human form, we can awaken to the recognition that all that Creation is, we are.

I had heard enthusiasm, promise, and humor in the voice of the Crusader when he asked, "When may I do it again?" There was only loving expectation for the next opportunity to present itself. The French Woman, in contrast to the Crusader, was in great emotional pain. Her reasons for leaving the body were merely to be rid of her pain. The Crusader wanted to free his consciousness from its form to begin his next adventure. His expectation was contagious because for a moment I, too, felt the same appreciation for this human life I was living.

The implication was astounding! The Crusader lived before the French Woman and the Child in the monastery and, of course, before me. Yet, they were all "me." He was where he was in consciousness a thousand years ago, while I am here still plodding along a spiritual path. Knowing with certainty that the Crusader was my own Being, I could only conclude that my concept of time and life was incorrect. That is, time must not be linear but more of a circle. Instead of having a beginning and an end, it had to be an uninterrupted circle. If that is so and we live within this circle of time (which is not time so much as Beingness), *all of us are enlightened Beings NOW.* All the awareness of Soul is available to us in our consciousness...*NOW.* What must we do to retrieve that awareness? After considerable thought, I could only conclude: *We must remember that this moment is the only moment there is. We are all that we are, or ever will be, right NOW, and we must behave according to that awareness.*

Chapter 9

GIFTS FROM THE MONASTERY CHILD

Before working on this book, the story of the Child in the monastery had no far-reaching significance for me. I felt her despair, of course, but unlike the French Woman or the Crusader, I did not become one with her. I merely observed her and sent her a message. She gave a chronological continuity to these past lives and I felt that this was her only significance.

When it came time to write about the Monastery Child for this book, I had to enter my notes into the computer and proceed with the analysis. During this process the experience deepened and a new appreciation for it took hold. Several times during the editing, waves of emotion flooded over me. The more I worked on the story, reading and editing, the stronger the emotion grew. After a couple of hours at the computer, I was so restless that I had to stop working.

After all these years I thought I would recognize a signal when I got one. The signal had almost always been an odd sensation much like an emotion, but more like a change in energy vibration. It may seem that I cry easily and often in these experiences, but the tears were a way of coping with the increase of subtle energies. These energies allowed my consciousness to become more refined, raising it to a level where the invisible becomes visible or at least comprehensible. What I called emotion in these experiences was actually a purifying of consciousness, and I did that through tears. Another person might achieve the same results some other way more compatible with their nature, such as pacing, sleeping, or even shaking.

Finally recognizing emotion as a signal, I sat quietly and said aloud, not to a person but to my feelings of restlessness, "Okay, what is it? Is there something you want to tell me? I accept you. I appreciate you. I value you. You are a part of me so, please, if there is something, tell me."

I waited, expecting to see a picture on my inner screen. None came. Instead, I could *feel* the Child from the monastery. I couldn't see her, yet I felt her presence, only now she was no longer a child but a mature being. I heard her say, "Thank you."

"What for?" I asked.

Then she impressed upon me, as a complete thought, this information: If she and I had not connected with one another, if she had not sensed my presence and then seen me, she would have languished in the hell of her own creation when she died. It might have been many, many years (as we measure time) before she could have freed herself or before others could have helped her out of this after-life hell. I had entered into her conscious experience and she had responded by forgiving herself and quite literally saving herself.

After receiving this information, I was a bit confused and thought, "I don't understand."

I heard her reply as she read my thoughts: "I am you and you are me." I sensed the smile in her words as I felt her leave.

How was I to interpret this exchange? There was so much to say, but are there even words to express it? What was meant by the "hell of her own creation"? How could she have "seen" me when she lived in the 14th century and I in the 20th? What allowed such an exchange to take place? Who am I that this should happen to me? Who are the "others" she referred to as helping her in hell? How could one "enter into" another's consciousness? I sensed that there was a deeper meaning to her remark, "I am you and you are me," than simply a past-life memory, but what? Was there something else she was trying to tell me?

I searched for the answers in my heart and mind. I asked my inner spiritual teachers for help and guidance in understanding the purpose of this experience and, once understood, incorporating it into my life.

Almost two years went by, two years of shifting, discarding, expanding, and the imparting of new awareness. And I have no doubt that the answers I have today will also be expanded and altered as more and more Truth enters my conscious awareness, not that what is written here is not the Truth, so much as not the whole Truth. It is not the whole Truth because I am not yet conscious of my whole (holy) self or my God-Self. But I, like most people, am in the process of *becoming* aware of my wholeness, so with that in mind, let's begin with the easiest question first.

What allowed such an exchange to take place? I would have to say *openness*. The child in her despair was open to intervention at a spiritual level. I was open to spiritual impulse and willing to respond by being still and meditative. Both our responses were synchronized to allow the experience to happen.

Actually, similar things happen to us in our daily lives. For example, have you ever started down a particular street and on an impulse decided to take another route? Then you found yourself meeting up with someone you hadn't seen in a long time whom you wouldn't have seen if you hadn't responded to the impulse. The odd thing is, as you talked with this person you learned that he, too, had changed his route on impulse. Thus two people connected by following their inner direction.

What was meant by the "hell of her own creation"? Like this child, many of us create hell right here on Earth through our perceptions. We all have our own perceptions of life, death, people, events, and circumstances. Where do these perceptions come from? They come from our beliefs. What we believe determines our reality, or what we consider to be real. Change our beliefs and we change the way we see ourselves and our world. We act according to our beliefs. Then our actions and our beliefs *become* that which is real to us (our *personal* reality).

The Monastery Child was bound by the beliefs of her time. Therefore she felt that severe punishment was not only destined but justified. You and I know that today life is more flexible. By today's standards, whatever that child could have done would not warrant the severe punishment she placed upon herself or felt that God would have cast upon her. What made the rules and mores of her day different? Nothing changes from century to century except our beliefs. People don't change, "sin" doesn't change, but the way we look at people and circumstances does change. Our perceptions have softened, our hearts have opened, and our minds have become more understanding. Throw these ingredients into the pot of life and we brew up new ways of looking at things and new sets of beliefs.

Through some transgression she thought that she had committed, the child believed she had "let God out of her life." She was so consumed with the ramifications of losing God that her actual transgression was lost to me. I have no idea what "sin" this Child believed she had committed. In fact, since I was privy to her thoughts, I knew she gave no thought to the offense itself but was totally consumed with guilt, contrition, and punishment.

Her beliefs in a punishing God and a God of retribution were shattered when she received the message that I was her future and that she would continue to grow and evolve. I believe when the Child saw or sensed me, I became whatever her perception of salvation was at that time. She could have perceived me as an angel, as the "Blessed Mother," or even as herself forgiven and living in "heaven." Whatever her vision was, it allowed her to forgive herself and to rise in awareness to another level of understanding where she could see that she existed beyond her sense of the physical world. Through her revelation she became aware that there was an eternal quality of her being that transcended the events of this world.

We all have spiritual guides and teachers who help us in our search for Truth. Mine often give me specific lessons and answer questions when they deem necessary. The following journal entry was received in meditation and bears relevance to the Child's experience:

"Do you not see that man has grown so accustomed to expecting punishment before reward [spiritually], and so accustomed to not knowing a loving God that most of man's rites, ceremonies, and [religious] customs and beliefs involve sacrifice and suffering? THIS IS NOT TRUE. You have seen us and do know us [my spiritual teachers]. You know we did not arrive at our state of awareness through pain and suffering but were brought forth from a Consciousness of love. Therefore remember ALL ARE A CREATION OF LOVE. Mankind grows by and through love. Any belief that has anywhere in it a need, an expectation, or a duty to suffer or experience pain is ERRONEOUS, built upon superstition, and as such, must be discarded so that mankind may get on with its divine business."

This message reinforces the idea that beliefs are just that— beliefs *about* truth and reality, and not necessarily a Truth or Spiritual Reality. I've learned that we must be willing to surrender our beliefs in order to go forward spiritually. We can surrender these beliefs gracefully or surrender them kicking and screaming. That is our choice. But if we remember that we are Spiritual Beings by *creation* and human beings by *belief*, it might be easier to release our limitations.

If the Child in the monastery had been unwilling or unable to surrender her belief in an unforgiving God, she would indeed have languished in hell. A hell created by an omnipresent God? Impossible! Since God is all-present, hell would have to be Godly. Therefore it could not be hell. It would have to be the hell which *she believed existed* and which she created from the beliefs of her culture.

We could examine own lives and ask, "What beliefs am *I* holding onto that are inconsistent with the existence of an all-present, all-powerful, and all-loving God? What hell have I created for myself, my family, or my enemy? Perhaps this idea of creating our own hell from our perceptions may seem a bit abstract, but this is not so. We need only to think back over all the times we projected our perceptions onto situations and suffered needlessly.

It is because we are Spirit Being that sooner or later we will awaken to the vastness of our True Selves. We may choose to awaken through expanding our awareness and living in a more conscious state of being, or we may choose to awaken through pain and suffering. This may sound melodramatic but how many of us, myself included, have had to go through a drastic condition—illness, loss, or lack—before we finally emerged "better for the experience"? Haven't you said at least once in your life, "That was a terrible ordeal but I learned so much that it was worth it"?

Hopefully this book says that you can, you may, and you are meant to learn through expanding your awareness of spiritual Truth. Even the tiniest grain of Truth active in your awareness can save eons of misery. When you perceive Spiritual Reality in this life, you will no longer have to learn through pain and suffering.

I have put this to use in my own daily life by pausing to reflect on each given challenge. How much of this problem or condition is my perception built on belief and how much of it reflects my awareness of Truth? A little spiritual Truth in your everyday existence means that you do not react to the outer world as if you had no control or power.

I am reminded of a time a few years ago when I went to a reputable and competent doctor for a somewhat minor though troublesome complaint. While he was examining me, I could see he was agitated. He questioned me about an exam I'd had two years previously and determined that the other doctor had been careless. "Why had I let this condition go on so long?" he scolded. He finished the exam and spoke alarmingly of cancer, the size of a tumor, and the various complications due to its size.

I was to report immediately to the hospital for an ultrasound; an emergency operation was needed. He then left the room abruptly, uttering something about going at once to make arrangements

I was alone in the examination room, sitting on a cold, hard table dressed only in a paper gown. I asked myself, "What am I feeling? Am I fearful? Alarmed? Anxious? Angry?" I realized I was feeling none of those things. I was feeling just ordinary.

The doctor, who represented an authority, had just listed a series of dangers, including cancer. He spoke with urgency, alarm, and concern about my well-being (or lack of). I realized he could have said, "Isn't it a lovely day?" and I would have felt the same.

As I dressed and prepared to follow through with the designated tests, I knew I had just claimed a portion of my spiritual liberty. There was a part of me, an inner knowing, that recognized that this condition had nothing to do with "Me." It may concern my body but not that inner me. The doctor was agitated but I was fine.

I was fine because I was aware that my life and body are *mine*, subject to *my* awareness of Truth active within *my* Consciousness. It may have been true for the doctor that what he had perceived as a dangerous condition was indeed serious. That was not my belief or my truth. Therefore I did not give my power of well-being over to him. It would have been easy, had I not been grounded in Truth, to *react* to the doctor's findings and expand on that fear and all the possibilities surrounding surgery and cancer. That did not happen because when you know even a little bit of Truth, you are *no longer at the mercy of other people, conditions, or authority.* You are your *own* authority.

I went on to get a second opinion, even after the tests came back agreeing with the first doctor's diagnosis. I chose the second surgeon because he agreed to three conditions. First that there would be no negative comments made about my condition while I was under anesthesia, regardless of what they found; second, that the anesthesiologist would speak to me during the operation, telling me how quickly I would heal and how well I was; and third, that I would not have to eat hospital food. He told me to expect a five- to seven-day admission and to plan on six to eight weeks for recovery.

My beliefs at that time were simple: "I" was not ill. My body might be under siege, but it was not a "power," just a temporary condition. The doctors did not have the power to make me well or make me worse. All authority was in my own Consciousness of Truth. This was an opportunity for me to practice living what was, at that time, my highest awareness of spiritual Consciousness. I went into the operation grateful for the chance to exercise my dominion. The results were remarkable.

Of course, there was a huge tumor which took hours to remove, but it was benign. I was home in two and half days and Christmas shopping with my mom within seven days. I had no pain beyond an occasional twinge, no after-effects, and no problems. This, I believe, was because I chose to live my own Truth, that I am Spiritual Being not just human being, and that I will *not* give authority and hence, power, to someone else regardless of their qualifications. Do you see how practical, how easy, and how normal it is for each of us to take our lives back from false notions and limited awareness? Remember, your perception is *your* perception, nobody else's. Therefore, you may *choose* to seek the truth about SELF, or you may choose to be influenced and controlled by the beliefs and superstitions of others.

The remaining few questions regarding the Monastery Child (such as, "How could she see me?" and "What others could help her in hell?") were resolved as I explored the concept of time. We may confine our attention to a time span of seventy or eighty years, thinking that birth and death define us. We are so busy with worldly activity that we forget that there is an "I" that is doing the thinking, causing the action, and breathing the body. That "I" is our spiritual Consciousness. That "I" does not change, does not die, does not get born; it just *IS*. It is that "I" that remembers being born, remembers asking to be born. That "I" is the Truth of our Being.

The Monastery Child lived in the 14th century. The Truth that was the Truth in the 14th century is the same Truth in the year 2000. Individual perception is the only variable. The world has always been round. It was round before Columbus "discovered" it was round, and it will continue to be round for the remainder of its life as we know it.

What was it that kept people of the 15th century from sailing forth to uncharted worlds? It was simply a *perception* that the world was flat. Such an erroneous perception did not limit or effect the world's roundness. It did, however, keep *those who believed it was flat* in a minuscule world, held captive by the sight of the sky meeting the ocean. The sky never does touch the ocean. All the believing in the world will not make it touch. It took the willingness and courage of a few to shatter that belief and open a vast "new world." And so it is with our spiritual discovery.

We must not, we cannot, be defined solely by our physical senses. We must be willing to sail forth, guided by our inner spirit and the lives and experiences of those who have chartered expanding awareness through the ages. Then we can discover *our* "new world." As with America, we will find it is not a "new" world at all. Until Columbus made Europe aware of it, America did not exist for them; until you become *conscious* of your own divinity, in a sense it does not exist for you.

For the Child in the monastery, the only thing that could change was her perception of God and sin. She suffered terribly because she believed in a punishing God. What we can see now is that her belief could not change what is, or change the Truth. It was her *perception* that caused her to suffer, not God. Once she was able to perceive something of the infinite nature of God and of her spirit Self, her awareness expanded, as did her perception, which in turn changed her life and her reality.

The fact that she came back at a later time as a more mature being to thank me also raises the issue of time being nonlinear. It is not impossible or unusual that we can have simultaneous experiences. (Remember the example of having a headache and balancing the checkbook, etc.) Simultaneous experiences mean that we, as infinite Consciousness, are not limited by time and space; we exist concurrently in our awareness.

To illustrate this concept, take a pencil and draw a circle. Then enclose a small section of the circle's circumference with brackets. The circle represents your infinite Consciousness. It has no beginning and no end. The space between the brackets represents a life experience; for example, this lifetime that you're living now.

Look at the circle and the brackets. Simply because there are brackets does not mean that the circle is broken or incomplete, or even separate from any other bracketed part. All parts of the circle still exist, even with the brackets. In fact, there are many sets of brackets in our infinite circle. Because our perceptions as human beings are limited to time and space, we are conscious of only one experience at a time, or one set of brackets at a time. As we expand our perceptions, we are able to "view" more than one set of brackets.

This may sound a bit radical because we are used to thinking within the limits of our concept of time, the physical senses, and a mind confined by only what it can rationally understand. It is only when we cling to our beliefs about self, time, space, and what we can logically understand that such an explanation seems impossible. I know from my own experience it is *not* impossible. Nor should it be unusual. Who told us to limit our consciousness? Why is it considered strange to expand awareness beyond the five physical senses? Why do we have to die to have these experiences?

Truly, I do not know where our sense of limitation came from. I only know that it is not our true nature. It could not be. Since the beginning of recorded history, men and women have tried to tell us we are more than our physical selves. I suppose it is easier to expand our awareness when we experience that state called dying because we lose that personal sense of ourselves that identifies us as "my" body, "my" feelings, "my" mind.

When we lose that personal identity, we become more vast. We pass through those windows in consciousness that look out into infinity, leaving behind the limited personal self and expanding into the Self. The personal self considers its life to depend on "my heart beating, my brain thinking, my body functioning." When we have a "death experience," we recognize we no longer have a brain, a body, or a beating heart but we are aware that I *am still* "I," *consciousness, soul, spirit.*

If you were on an operating table and a surgeon cut you open "from stem to stern," could the doctor find *you* anywhere in there, or take *you* out of your body to put *you* somewhere else? Could he even recognize *you* with his physical senses? If you donated your heart to another at your death, would that mean the recipient would become *you,* since it is your heart that beats in that other body? Of course not. And why? Because the "I" of you, the "Being" of you, the "Soul" of you is that unlimited, invisible, eternal Consciousness which *you are.* It is not your physical self or physical organs.

It is because we are this eternal, infinite Consciousness that I was able to enter into the experience of the Child in the monastery, and she in turn was able to come to thank me. Such an exchange could not have occurred within the confines of "normal" human awareness. This is also the reason why we can help those whom we consider to be dead. When we understand that Spirit Being doesn't die but only changes the way it "dresses" in physical bodies, then we can be assured that our prayers, our love, our loving thoughts reach those who have departed. Therefore, the mature Child was referring to the prayers for the dead as the "others who could have helped her."

We must free ourselves from measuring our existence as only the years between birth and death. Through the ages people have sought various methods of experiencing this freedom through drugs, fasting, and near-death experiences to name a few. The most effective and conservative approach, I believe, is meditation.

Through meditation the human mind is quieted, and then our Divine nature can exert Itself. I was able to enter into the Child's experience partly because, through meditation, my mind stopped focusing on worldly distractions and expanded to a more limitless awareness of being. In such a state, I was open to the cry for help. Also, the Child was so repentant, so desperately looking for help from God, that she was able to transcend her humanness and raise her awareness to discern a level of Consciousness that is timeless, formless, and limitless. It was a moment when both she and I were open to infinite intervention. It is not that I am special, gifted, or even unusual. I am just a regular person who, through the study of Truth and meditation, has been able to expand my awareness and, on occasion, access the endless invisible Consciousness that we all are.

This Consciousness is a web that connects us with all souls, "alive" or "dead." When prayers are spoken in truth and love, they are active energy that can be heard, understood, and used by any consciousness that is receptive. If we know the Truth, that we and everyone else are Divine Spirit, then at no time and under no circumstances are any of us without help, love, or support. We are always able to rectify a past wrong regardless of whether a person is "alive" or "dead." Consciousness is what we are. We are never dead, nor are we ever unconscious (without Consciousness).

It is important to remember that whatever is possible for one soul is possible for all because there is only *one source of creation—God, the Creative Principle; one material to create with—God-substance; and one divine Creation—infinity expressing as God-being—as you, as me, as every living thing.*

In order to live in the unlimited Consciousness that we already are, we must be willing to discard our limited *beliefs*. This is the most important thing we can do for ourselves. Our *awareness* of Truth is a living organic entity, constantly growing, transforming, and evolving. Truth does not change. Our ability to recognize and live the Truth is constantly changing if we let it. If awareness didn't shift, we wouldn't grow. What allowed these experiences to take place was my willingness to continually discard what no longer served my expanding inner awareness. It isn't as hard as you may think; just relax and let yourself *remember all that you are.*

SECTION 11

"There are more things in heaven and Earth...than are dreamt of in your philosophy."

— Shakespeare
Hamlet Act I

PREFACE

L et me introduce this section by saying that at the time I felt the following events to be incredible. For several days afterward, I would reflect on them and ask, "Was I dreaming? Did this really happen?" My mind would race over the events, questioning everything. I would begin to doubt. If I could quiet my mind and become still, I would ... I am ... flooded with the awareness and the assurance of the reality of these experiences. I cannot explain why these things happened as they did, or even how such things could happen. I can only relate them imperfectly. I say imperfectly because words are excruciatingly inadequate. The nuances, the colors, the energy of what you are about to read were so far beyond the power of mere words that the experience is diminished greatly by the telling.

Once again I ask you not to judge these next few pages or dissect them intellectually but read them for what they are—one person's interpretation of the Infinite Invisible. How do I know that this was a true and spirit-gifted experience? Because it has radically and completely changed who and what I thought I was. A large part of me died in the following experiences and a new, more compassionate, more expansive person was born.

Chapter 10

REVELATIONS

The memories revealed so far have been an important aspect of my spiritual journey. Not only did they confirm the eternal nature of Spirit, but they served to expand my consciousness. Even now they continue to unfold and impart their treasures in an enduring way. I realize that those memories and events of the past were a preparation for a dynamic series of connected revelations.

This story unfolds over several meditations, beginning many years ago with a brief incident. One morning I lay in bed awake but feeling lazy. Gazing down the hallway into the opposite end of the house, I saw a fire-red sphere suspended in mid-air at the far end of the hallway. My eyes were wide open. I watched it, caught between disbelief and fascination, for I had never seen such a phenomenon before. It began to move steadily toward me, silently, an intense red. As it came closer, I began to feel uncomfortable, uncertain, and then afraid. In retrospect, I realize I was afraid of the unknown and not the occurrence itself. By the time the sphere had reached the doorway of my bedroom, I was reciting a protection mantra I had stored in the back of my mind years ago but never had occasion to use. Suddenly the image disappeared. Fifteen years later it would show itself again, this time as a prelude to a life-altering experience.

I am an alert meditator. That is to say, in meditation, my senses and awareness of the physical world become heightened. For example, if I had flowers in the kitchen (which is on the other side of the house with two sets of doors between), I could smell the flowers in meditation. Although my physical senses are sharp, they don't interfere with my meditation. They are only an awareness, not a distraction. I say this because I want you to under-

71

stand that although I was in a meditative state during these experiences, I was wakeful, fully conscious, and quite myself.

Years later in meditation the red fiery globe showed itself once again, looking as it did all those years ago except for the addition of white-gold rings circling it like the rings of the planet Saturn. Such a vision may seem a bit odd at first, but remember that when we tap into areas outside our conditioned experiences and frames of reference, our minds try to translate the new experience into words, pictures, and symbols to which we can relate. I saw a globe, fiery red in color, with circling rings because that was a symbol that I could decode into some form of understanding, albeit a wordless knowing or inner recognition. I would learn later as the experience imparted itself that there are no words, thoughts, or even symbols for the endless invisible realm of Spirit revealing Itself.

The sight of the globe did not frighten me this time. I felt a kind of pulsing warmth emanating from it that seemed distantly familiar. The red globe then began to appear many times in my meditations, hovering for just a short time and then disappearing. I had learned to accept it without any particular feeling. It never came close to me nor did it seem to move. It would simply materialize, then disappear.

One morning, this changed. The sphere appeared and began to spin. It drew close to me and the rings circling it spun over and through me. At once I felt the energy around me change. As the rings passed through me, an intense burning sensation went up my spine and over my head, making the area behind my eyes and nose sting with heat. All the bones in my face hurt and even my teeth felt on fire. A powerful, penetrating heat radiated out from the center of the palms of my hands, the back of my neck, and the soft spot on the top of my head.

As the fire moved through me, my entire body shook rapidly in a whirling motion. I became aware that here, as in all previous experiences, there was a moment I could choose to stop what was happening. I could jump out of the meditation, letting my rational mind pounce on these happenings, tear them apart, and label them foolishness and fancy. Or I could, and did, choose to relax and surrender into the experience. With that choice made, an inner directive impressed itself upon my mind to think the "Great Thought."

The "Great Thought" is my name for something I had read many, many years ago when I first became involved in metaphysics. It comes from the work of Baird Spalding, *Life and Teaching of the Masters of the Far East.*[1] The moment I read it, I dubbed it my "Great Thought" and considered it a most precious prayer.

Before I could focus completely on the "Great Thought," doubt entered my mind and I questioned, "Can this be my imagination? Is my mind playing some kind of trick?" Again, the command came, *"Rest...rest into this experience."* I concentrated on the "Great Thought" and spoke it silently as the experience continued: *"I stand steadfastly with my eyes fixed upon you, oh Father, knowing naught but you and seeing naught but God in all things."* As the rings spun close around me, I was able to see the core of the sphere. *"I stand firmly on the holy mount knowing naught but your life, your love and your wisdom, oh Father. Your divine spirit pervades me always, it surrounds me and abounds within and without me always."*

The sphere was like a giant world, bright red, yellow, and white hot. *"This I know is not for me alone, oh Father, but is for all your children, for I know I have naught but only that which all have."* The sudden and extraordinary realization filled me that this globe was a great Being and I **knew** this Being.

"And there is naught but God for all. I thank you, Father."

A love and deep longing filled me, as it does even now as I recount this experience. The love itself was tangible. I felt it ripple through me to the bone. I thought, "Could this be a dream?" The Being spoke with a voice that would have terrified me had I not

[1] Life and Teaching of the Masters of the Far East, Baird T. Spalding, Del Rey, CA, 1972

felt such love from it: *"You are experiencing the realm of eternity. You are expanding consciousness. Fear not, I have been with you since the beginning. Remember this."*

The experience ended, and I reveled in the wonder and awe of what had just occurred. I looked at the palms of my hands, half expecting to see charred centers from the burning sensation. There were none. I sat quietly for a time, then recorded the experience in my journal. As I wrote, it was difficult to fight back the tears. A passionate longing flooded me, a yearning that is with me even today, only with a greater understanding of purpose.

At the time, I wasn't sure what the words meant as I wrote in my journal, "What must I do to return? When will I be able to be with those I love?" But return where, and who was it that I loved? My rational mind didn't have the answers. Yet my heart knew that the place and beings of whom I wrote were my home and ancestry more than this Earth and my earthly family. How could such a thing be? I knew only that there was a profound need to unite with something both known and yet unknown to me.

In the months that followed, this "Being" came in and out of my meditations, becoming familiar and comforting and imparting to me many lessons, one of which is relevant to the experience:

"In human evolution only are you given the opportunity of temptation [choice] which lets you choose God above all things. But what is this "God"? It is that which is greater than you, but not separate from you. It is that which IS...IS LIFE...IS BEING...IS FOREVER AND EVER. That which is ever and always present and IT IS the ONLY...ONLY. Here in human form you are offered the opportunity to be and to consciously choose to be that which YOU ARE...DIVINE CHILDREN OF DIVINE CREATION."

As human beings, we are limited to our finite thoughts, processing and receiving information through the confines of the physical senses. If we limit awareness to our physical senses, then we will be *only* that—physical and finite, a three-dimensional being—when our true identity is multi-dimensional. God is infinite and therefore beyond my finite comprehension until those moments when Infinite Awareness breaks through the barriers of human consciousness. If we desire to have such moments, we must be willing to continually revise our old concepts and beliefs so that the new may reveal itself. This I was (and am) ready to do, so I welcomed the astounding revelation that was yet to come.

Months later, the "Being" appeared during a meditation without the rings around It. As I beheld it I was filled with intense love for this "Being" and felt it loving me back with equal intensity. As I write these words, they cannot begin to express what I felt. I can only say that in that moment I saw *MY* God, and how I sprang from this God. I *knew* when I saw It that not everyone in my life and in my world came from this same God. I understood that the purpose of my (or anyone's) springing from God was to go forth into experience and evolve into their own God, who in turn sends parts of Itself out to repeat the process, ad infinitum. This was astonishingly clear and very profound. (I seriously considered leaving this last revelation out because I didn't know if the concept was lucid enough to express clearly. I can only say that this is true for me, unmistakable and of enormous significance. I am so grateful for having been shown this.)

I was euphoric. Later that day, my husband wanted to know what had happened to me. He kept saying that I looked and seemed different. He could not say how, only that I was different and that my actual appearance had changed. Such an observation from my husband warrants mentioning. He is not always observant of his surroundings or those around him, preferring to dwell in the mental corridors of equations and theorems. I might paint a large pastel-colored living room dark teal and it would be days before he would say, "The room looks a little different." I was certain of an inner change after my experience, but my husband's observation confirmed an outer change as well.

The feelings of euphoria shifted over the next thirty-six hours, a shift that shattered all concepts of myself, the people in my life, and my way of relating to the God of my understanding. For the first time in my life, I felt I had no footing, no foundation. I suddenly felt as though I had woken up from amnesia and had to start living at some random point. As if life had been going along fine, but then one day you begin to remember who you really are, where you came from, and who your family is. You feel shocked, unsettled, yet at the same time there is a sense of excitement and gratitude.

Most of us have an idea of who we think we are and what God is—concepts that for us seem to be accurate. I was no exception. In fact, I was very comfortable with my concepts. I didn't think they needed to be changed, just expanded. Of course, I should have known better. The true spiritual seeker is *never* allowed to linger in passiveness or stagnation. The revelation itself was both complex and irrevocable. Put quite simply, I realized my concepts of God and spirituality had to undergo a radical lobotomy. I had no choice since that brief vision totally demolished all I thought I knew or even faintly understood. I have since realized that as long as I am searching for Truth, this shattering action is a necessary part of that search. The purpose of such action is not to destroy *us*, but rather to shatter the *beliefs* we harbor that keep us eclipsed in the midst of a radiant universe.

As the days passed, I adjusted to this new idea of "many Gods." These are Creator Beings creating life in their image, rather than the ancient idea of different gods to be worshipped and prayed to for their gifts. "The Life" they create undergoes eons of experience and evolution until it becomes inclusive enough to create life in its *own* image...and on and on through all time. The word "image" here does not refer to a physical or material state. It denotes energetic likeness. We may all share a common form—two arms, two legs, and one head—yet our intrinsic energy may be quite different from one another.

In the days following, I felt a shadow around my heart as though a tall building had crumbled to the ground, sending up clouds of dust and debris. That dust made me restless, melancholy, and unable to focus. I was unable to sift through the rubble of my razed beliefs. I would feel myself try to get a footing, but I would sink back into the wreckage of shattered feelings, thoughts, and meaningless words. Somewhere in my core, I knew *Oneness* would be my lifeline but I couldn't seem to connect with it through my clouded thoughts and feelings.

I needed someone who could help shift the energies around me and the name came to mind of someone who was an expert in subtle energy and its workings. Locating him demonstrated, once more, how the universe supports our awakening spirit. Unknown to me he had been living abroad for years, yet only weeks before I needed his expertise, he had moved back to Atlanta.

Impatient about settling my mind and heart, I met JD at his house with not the least suspicion of what was about to transpire. We talked for a short time and I felt comfortable that this was the right place and the perfect person to help me integrate energy. For the work to begin, JD had me lie comfortably on some cushions. He then asked me to remember what I considered to be my most important past-life memory.

That was the easy part, for I had considered the memory of the Crusader to be the most significant, since it had revealed that linear time did not exist in Spirit. My thoughts went to the Crusader, expecting to explore a deeper understanding of time, but I found that my focus was on the Crusader personally, rather than on the issue of time. The question seemed to be why he had gone to the Holy War when he really did not want to. As I listened and felt him in my inner awareness, he began to identify his reasons for joining the Crusades.

He had been for many years the student and friend of a monk. This ascetic was a man of great scholarship, powerful devotion, and piety. The monk had encouraged and indeed expected the

Crusader to join the war. The Crusader loved and respected his teacher above all men.

At this moment, I felt my consciousness merge with the Crusader's. His thoughts were now my thoughts, there was no longer a "he" and a "me," just one awareness.

The Crusader was what we would call a free-thinker. He held many views and ideas in his heart that were radical for men of his day. Those thoughts he kept hidden within himself, along with a sense of guilt for his inner beliefs. He felt himself a heretic at times and unworthy of the monk's fellowship since he could not seem to muster the religious zeal his teacher espoused. Certainly what the Crusader considered heretical was really tolerance. In the mind of his teacher, a devout monk, tolerance could only be translated as the Devil's work. Here I saw the beauty and gentleness of the Crusader's soul, but also his lack of spiritual confidence.

Because of this inner insecurity, the Crusader looked to the monk in matters of religion and morality. He relied on the monk's guidance and trusted him without question. As this information unfolded within my consciousness, and as I experienced the Crusader's mind and nature, at that moment we both realized simultaneously that he had acted against his own inner voice by joining the Holy War. He knew in his soul such a quest was not natural for his spirit and that he had followed his teacher's bidding *rather than trusting his own inner-self*. He had done *man's* will and not God's. Feelings of self-doubt and spiritual insecurity had kept him from realizing his own spiritual fullness in that lifetime. Through his experiences, the Crusader had come to recognize he was Spirit Being living as a human being, yet he had been unable to incorporate that truth into his life. He had not developed the inner trust and confidence to act in accordance with his own "knowing."

I was conscious of both myself and the Crusader simultaneously, I saw my life as it is now and his life as it was then. Both the Crusader and I had been privy to spiritual Truth in our respective lives. We had experienced Spirit, seen it in action, and recognized it. Yet both of us had been afraid to step forward and act in accordance with that recognition which would have led us to fulfillment. I felt his sense of being separate from the beliefs of his time and knew that he had been able to cope with it only because of the friendship with and respect of his teacher. He had been unwilling to risk that friendship for what he had believed to be true.

This was a wonderful moment of acknowledgment and love, and a deep sense of appreciation for his soul filled me. I remembered how I, in this life, almost did the same thing with regard to friends and teachers. Gratefully, I had found the strength to act in harmony with my inner guidance, regardless of the beliefs of those I loved and respected.

Throughout this experience, I was unaware of JD. I cannot remember if he asked me questions or if I spoke aloud. Then, as if in the distance, his voice posed the next question: "What is before the Crusader that is important to you?"

Suddenly, my surroundings evaporate. I become aware of my Self as part of something much larger, consciousness without material form, watching the Earth create itself. I see swirling masses of colored gases, stars, and moons. Gradually the planet Earth materializes. Like a video tape on fast forward, it spins through rain, sun, ice, and fire. Then there is a cacophony of color and a myriad of tones that I "see" but know to be sound, not sight (the senses of sight and sound are not separate but are a unified sense).

My response as this unfolds is total enchantment, like watching a potter create something beautiful on the wheel—a lump of clay one minute and a superb piece of art the next. I am acutely aware that this watching consciousness is ME. I am there, my form like fluid crystal, a liquid hologram with many, many dimensions. But I am still me, my same consciousness. I feel blissfully happy, incredibly perfect, and "right."

With great curiosity, I watch life unfold on the planet. Humans appear. I am fascinated to watch them walk. JD asks me to describe what I see. I hear his voice in some distant recess in my mind, but I do not reply. I just want to watch (I am in rapture at watching a human form standing upright and walking, with arms moving and a rhythm all its own.)

For a while, I am lost in the wonder of the human body and its movement, all parts of the body acting in beautiful obedience. I have a sense of awe for the "container" (body) and how it gets everything to perform in concert with such grace in so confined a space. I wonder, What would it be like? Could I do such a thing, be so contained and make it move?

Within seconds of watching the emergence of Man, I found myself attached to an old man. JD asks what I'm seeing and I say I am an old man, but I am not really him. Somehow I am able to "attach" myself to him. Through the Old Man, I am able to experience human existence but I am not really him, nor am I human.

We are living in what seems to be a highly technical culture. Eons have passed since that first sighting of mankind. People are traveling in, or more accurately as, vehicles. People seldom walk anymore. They travel in an odd kind of pod that is both separate from the traveler and one with him. I see a person standing straight, then a covering appears from behind his shoulders and folds over him; a smaller covering appears at his feet. When he is covered, he moves rapidly, faster than I can follow with my vision.

Through this Old Man, I work closely with animals and especially plants. It is an experience and acquaintance I have never known before. They are called plants but really they are beings as we are beings, with all the characteristics and possibilities that all life has. Plants and animals can communicate and plants have feelings, not as emotions but as awareness. They communicate love and are teaching the Old Man many things. This is not done through words but through a kind of pulsing of information.

I work tenaciously to gather new experiences and information from the plants and animals and love the opportunity. I feel the same as I did when I saw the Earth being formed. That is, I feel "right" and somewhat childlike in the ever new adventures of each moment with the Old Man. I have little or no contact with other humans, mostly because they do not interest me and also because the Old Man seems to shun human contact.

I am aware of a young girl, perhaps a relative of the Old Man, who loves him. She comes in and out of our environment at will. The

Old Man seems to accept her and her lighthearted love but cares most deeply and passionately for his plants and animals. His huge household is contained within an invisible energy field similar to glass, only much finer, yet with structure and mass.

I do not know how much time I spend in this experience with the Old Man. It seems like a very long time, as there is so much information and so many things to try and do. I especially learn to care for and admire the plant world. They are like wise brothers and sisters to me. The animals are also very precious. I consider them to be not only wise but totally unconditional in their love. The thing that strikes me the most in my present consciousness is that the plant and animal kingdoms (as we refer to them today) are not less than myself but simply different. There is no sense of one or the other being more evolved or on a higher plane.

As I am working, there comes a great upheaval. Everything seems to crumble. The energy field shatters all around us. The plants are demolished. The animals are destroyed as the very ground erupts all around us. Chaos is everywhere. I become separated from the Old Man. I am aware that this is a human-induced cataclysm. War they call it. In a flash, I perceive the history leading to this event. It stems from a struggle for power, competition gone awry, destruction in order to control. I see this but find it hard to fathom. Why would Man destroy something he could not own simply because he was unable to possess it? Isn't experiencing it enough? Men were destroying each other deliberately!

I feel confusion, deep sorrow, and pain. These were sensations unknown to me until that moment. I think, "Why can't they do the right thing, the higher thing? Why must there be this contention?" I make a pronouncement: "THIS IS WRONG!"

Instantly, it is as if a great iron cage clamps down over me. I hear the clanging sound echo through long corridors of space as it encases me. I am, in that instant, a prisoner of human evolution. I am entombed, totally confined, feeling dreadful things I had no idea existed, for they never existed in my awareness until that moment. Feelings of complete limitation, injustice, and fear. How could this be happening to me? Where did these feelings come from? And why...why...why must I now be so restrained?

Truly there were no words to convey that incredible horror. In a moment I was aware of being in JD's house. I was conscious of me as myself in this life but the despair, the total outrage of my soul was unappeasable, my tears rampant. I felt my face red hot with the injustice of my sentence and could only wrap my arms around myself and rock back and forth and cry, "It isn't fair! It's not fair! One mistake and I am here for eternity."

Again, our language is completely inadequate to describe the feelings in that moment's recognition. I wanted out, another chance. How could this have happened? In the most excruciating pain I have ever known, I cried uncontrollably.

JD let me cry for a while before asking, "Do you know what you did?"

"Yes...I *judged!* I pronounced judgment."

JD continued to speak to me about the experience. Caught up in the anguish of the memory, I was only half listening. His voice was a droning sound on the periphery of my awareness until he mentioned "interim time." He was referring to the time between lifetimes, the period during which the soul examines and evaluates the life just lived. Here the soul scrutinizes lessons learned and unlearned.

I had never thought about "where" such a soul-review would take place but, according to JD, it was a kind of "neutral zone," peopled with Beings of Light that act as counselors and advisors.

Then something he said made me sit up straight and interrupt him. I stated with absolute authority, "No! No, I don't do that. I am able to return to my eternal family, my true home, my own evolution." It was not clear to me why I was able do this. I only knew that I could and that after a time, either I was compelled or chose to return to this Earth experience to complete the learning.

I realize the above paragraph may raise many questions regarding what does happen in those periods between incarnations. I only know that for me, I was able to return "home." Strange though it may sound, I have no explicit knowledge of where or what home I was alluding to. However, all my life I have had a real and palpable connection with something I identified as "home."

In the days following this experience, I appraised my life and found myself not measuring up. I had come to view enlightenment as a series of stages. First, we know the Truth. Next, we must recognize that we *are* that Truth. Then that recognition must be *realized*. It must become *real* to us. That is, all that we *know* we are must be lived and expressed in order to become masters of our selves. What we are *without* must be as we are *within*.

I looked at myself and my life and felt enlightenment to be an impossible goal. I became frustrated and self-critical. I was striving to be less judgmental in how I viewed my world and fellow inhabitants, but everything I did and saw was being filtered through my heart's desire to "go home." The only moments of true comfort were in meditation when I would sense a connective link with my source. Every day as I looked around me I found it impossible to relate my heaven to this Earth. I was, in fact, growing more and more disconsolate.

Thankfully all this changed with the help of those invisible Beings who oversee and guide us on our chosen journey. It was a little over a month since I had worked with JD when I received the following meditation.

I see the Earth forming itself...all the stages of fire, ice, and beautiful crystals and colors. My consciousness is high, high above looking down. I am very expansive. I am everywhere. Slowly I begin to focus a small fraction of my self-awareness downward, becoming smaller and more concentrated. Abruptly, my awareness strikes a barrier surrounding the Earth. I know that this barricade is human consciousness, an energetic coagulation of beliefs, superstitions, ideologies, and concepts fashioned from human thought, action, and intention. It is through this obstruction that Pure Awareness must pass if It wishes to experience human existence. The coagulated energy adheres to Pure Awareness as It descends through the barrier. The effect is that Aware-

ness lowers Its vibration, darkens Its light, and becomes material.

At this moment, I recognize I am my own God. This God (Self) "speaks" rapidly and without words, communicating so quickly that my human mind cannot retain all that is pressed upon me. I do not try to remember what is given because the words given in Spirit are not important. Spirit is planting a seed in my awareness. That seed knows how, when, and what it is to do. I need only acknowledge and honor it and it will do the rest. I sit in the silence of communion and love for some time, not trying to understand but just feeling grateful.

In that state of gratitude, this teaching was given: "You are to be in this world...never can you be of it. You have been given this memory and experience because your heart was closing with grief and longing, whereas your work is to open the heart. All you know, where you live [in consciousness], who you are, all that you remember is yours for comfort. You must realize that the power and the science of Truth cannot be released into the world unleashed. It would shatter the heavily-laden form. It must be released slowly and cautiously. True, there are many ready to receive in greater measure, and so they are and will. But the world as such cannot. The work is to release Truth in small amounts. You know of the greater work and energy as do many, but as yet you may not release it in great measure.

Your knowing is meant for your comfort not for your confusion, so put it aside for now and be WHERE YOU ARE NOW.

I suddenly became aware of the same Hierarchy of Light Beings that I was with before birth.

It is true there is a destiny, but it is not as the world thinks. The destiny is that all will know they are God-I-AM, but the way to that attained destiny is not mapped out and may change second to second. It is best this way. Thus each becomes responsible [free will], so no one can say, when, who, or how in terms of human time, personalities, or experience. It may be that your work will complete itself before humanity can accept the full-

ness. If so, so be it. But it is also possible through the work of the many that humanity will be ready and then, of course, you will participate in the Great Release. This is not up to you, nor is it your work.

Know that you may return to this high vision at will. That will comfort you and you may find rest. However, be about the daily work and remain conscious. Your heart must remain open, but it cannot do so if you are frustrated and feeling inadequate with longing. Such emotions close the door of consciousness to your infinite nature which is GOD I AM...I AM GOD.

You are responsible for the work at hand. Stop trying. Just let this unfold. Remember, form is created through the immersion of high consciousness and thought. Consciousness is projected into form as an experience BUT IT IS NOT THE FORM. Consciousness has its own form, albeit invisible to human sense. Remember the agreement!"

"*I cannot,*" I say. "*I have tried but I don't remember...only that I wanted to do this.*"

"*You will remember in part, but do not dwell on this.*"

"*Please don't go,*" I say. "*Can't you stay longer and teach me more?*"

"*Go? Where could we go? Can Principle leave its Creation and separate Itself? Take the higher view.*"

Since this teaching I have been more content, better able to see in each day an opportunity to practice the Truth revealed to me through the years. A delicate understanding is shifting in my awareness as I let these experiences develop. I feel oddly older, more mature than I can ever remember.

Chapter 11

GIFTS FROM REVELATIONS

The latest revelation was so full, with many levels to be digested, that as I sat down to analyze what that experience revealed, it was hard to know where to begin. The moment I recognized "my" God and knew at that instant that there were many Gods, I was stunned, incredulous. Shocking as it was, the fullness of the idea did not immediately register. It was many days before the staggering significance of it hit me but now, curiously, as I prepare to analyze what was revealed, it no longer seems so shocking. Yet this revelation totally destroyed and disintegrated my concepts of, and relationship with, God. I was forced to rethink all that I believed and to throw away much of what I held to be true. Once I discarded all concepts and beliefs, I was left with only my lifeline: ONENESS. All else had to shift itself around. But if this were true, if there were many Gods, then what is this Oneness that remains when all else has been forsaken?

This Oneness is the One Creative Principle, the source from which the One, the Only, the Divine Substance emanates and originates. From this Substance all else is formed. It is the common source of everything existing, both visible and invisible, from angels to ashes. This Substance pervades whatever outline Divine Mind may draw, filling that framework with Spiritual Essence. In so doing, it naturally endows that form with Its own Divine Nature and Characteristics.

So, there are many Gods, with each evolution springing from its own particular God. In the moment that this vision was given to me, I could see, I could understand, and I knew with a knowing that was simply pure, that inherent in the One Creative Principle is Divine Diversity, which we interpret as God. This Principle is so infinite, so expansive, it is well beyond my cognitive understanding. The human mind can only filter it down in degrees of smaller and smaller units of comprehension until we end up with the God-concept of our limited understanding.

What is this "God" of our understanding? It is an *idea in mind* only. Why do I say that? Because God can neither be defined nor understood through human thinking. If you go looking for God in the world around you—in books, in teachers, or in teachings—you will not find It. God cannot be found, only *experienced*, but this experience cannot take place in a limited, finite, human mind. An Infinite Experience cannot be restricted to what we as humans wish to *believe*, what we wish to hold on to because we have been taught that something is so, or that God is a particular Being acting in a particular way. *God can and is meant to be experienced and_recognized within and as our own individual Consciousness.* But how and when?

The how may vary with each person. For many of us, one way is through *inner silence*, that state where our individual consciousness can swing far, far out into the infinite, into the invisible. The when is always the same for each of us: it is *now*. Having once intuited the Presence of something "unknowable but known," *we must be willing to abandon all past beliefs for this present awareness to unfold.*

What is meant by inner silence? The meaning is easy, actuality more difficult. Try sitting quietly without your mind dialoguing frantically. Not an easy thing to do, is it? The mind has reams of questions, millions of things for you to do, a host of opinions and judgments concerning just about everything in your life and it has a fear of silence. Developing the ability to still the mind-chatter produces inner silence.

In the diversity of the One Creative Principle there are many evolutions and many Gods, each one created of the common Substance. Each is different yet perfect and unique, and no one God is better than the others.

At the time this revelation was given me, it shook me to my very foundation. I didn't know who or what I was, why I was, or where I came from. My confusion became melancholy and bewildering. Yet I recognized that this was an orderly universe, like a cosmic kaleidoscope. Shake up the crystals and turn them around and the process looks chaotic, but no matter what you do, it produces a fine new orderly arrangement of light, color, and shape, the same substance re-formed anew. If I could be patient, if I could be trusting, then a new "world" would rise up.

Dear Reader, I, like many of you, was brought up with traditional religious doctrines. In those doctrines, God was something unattainable and mysterious. Any thought of more than one God belonged only to the ancient past and peoples of ignorance and darkness. I know if someone, even someone I trusted, had made the statements I have just made, I would have rejected them. I do not ask or expect you to accept this vision as true for you. I present it here as true *for me*. It is offered here because I have learned that whatever we *think* we know of God, or Life, or Being is *NEVER* it. God, Life, or Being can only be imparted through an experience of consciousness and awareness.

The experience itself is always *true*. It's when we try to understand or explain the experience that we begin to muddy the clear waters of our awareness because Pure Consciousness is beyond words, thoughts, or human comprehension. Why then have I tried to explain this in writing if it is impossible to understand? There are two reasons: first and foremost, because I was told to "tell the whole story" by my spiritual teachers; and second, because this experience has taught me that when Truth is imparted to you, no matter how disturbing or implausible it may seem at first, if it *is* the Truth it will settle into a harmonious expression of Spiritual Reality. If you are patient and open, you will see how a Truth feels true and how it functions in and for the Universal Good of all.

I believe this is the reality for anyone who experiences revelation. However, it may not be true for those with whom they share it. It often takes the power of the experience itself to break through our sense of limitation. For that reason, those who only hear about a vision may not receive all of its benefits. Of course, that need not be the case. I am writing of these events because anyone may receive the fullness of another's experience *if he or she is willing and able to surrender beliefs for an expanded view of that which Is.*

Because of the revelation of many Gods, I was led to JD and to that powerful experience regarding what I consider to be my entrance into the human scene. *Judgment...* all of these experiences, the past lives remembered and those not recalled, would never have taken place without *judgment.*

For a long time, I could not talk or write about that experience without tears and sadness. To have existed in completeness, perfection, and bliss as my true identity and then to lose it all in an instant was almost beyond endurance. Now months have passed and I have grown to love and appreciate that memory above all others. It is the most potent and the most promising because once we learn not to judge; when we no longer pronounce anything or anyone good or bad, we will not be good or bad either. At that point of neither good or bad, we will be "Being," pure and divinely whole (holy) in our awareness of Self, with all the fragments gathered up. We will see ourselves and others as we *are,* not as we imagine ourselves to be.

I cannot emphasize enough the consequences on the soul of passing judgment. I was shown, painfully and clearly, that at the moment we pass judgment we are so judged. Judged by whom, you may ask. By God? No, not any God, real or imagined, but by our very own Self. There is no super-being sitting up in the clouds somewhere passing judgment on mankind. There is, however, a Divine Principle that governs all things. When we live and move within this Principle, we live *as* this Principle in harmony. When we try to live outside of this Principle, we live in discord, limitation, and dis-ease. When we move outside of the Truth, we encounter conflict.

You may ask, is the Divine Principle creating the conflict in my life? To answer that, consider electricity. It is in our homes, in outlets in the walls, always present yet invisible. When we operate our appliances within the principle of electricity—that is, using the correct voltage with a proper cord and plug, the result is harmony, light, and activity. If we were to neglect the laws of electricity and drop a toaster into water and then plug it into an outlet, what would happen? Some shocking results! Who is to blame for the shock we receive? The electricity? Would electricity have suddenly taken a personal interest in us and decided to punish us? Of course not. Electricity is just being electricity; it does not punish us or reward us. It is completely impersonal. If we use our toaster correctly, the toast is not a reward but simply the result of operating within the principle of electricity.

So it is with life. When we operate within the integrity of the Divine Principle we then experience our Divinity. There is no punishment, no reward. Whatever our experience, good or bad, it is due to our awareness or ignorance of this Principle. Judgment is outside of Divine Principle. This Principle is All, *It is Whole* (holy). When we judge, we step outside of our Divine Wholeness (holiness) into a perceived separation.

In the experience with JD, I pronounced judgment on the human race. When I felt myself trapped as if in a cage, it was really the weight of human consciousness. In that experience, my consciousness perceived what it saw to be imperfect. That is, I saw something I did not comprehend (chaos and destruction) and in ignorance of the Principle of Oneness, passed judgment on it. That judgment was based upon an appearance, on what I discerned through sight, sound, and feeling. The minute I passed that judgment I *became* the state of consciousness that I judged. Whatever you judge, you are destined to become and live. *Consciousness is what you are conscious of or aware of. If you are NOT conscious of good or bad (pairs of opposites), then you CANNOT experience them!*

Up until that moment of pronouncement, I lived in a world of Oneness: diversity but *not separation*. Plants and animals are *different from*, but not judged better or lesser, than I. They are an aspect of the wholeness of my Self Awareness. Humanity chooses to learn and grow through contrast, through experiencing pairs of opposites. The minute I accepted *opposites* rather than *differences* into my awareness, I became destined to experience human existence.

I am sure that if I had accepted the feeling of being trapped in human consciousness and had not judged the condition good or bad but viewed it as an experience in the "moment," I would have been "free" again. I would have returned to the Consciousness of Oneness. I did not do that, but went on to judge my situation as unfair, which further perpetuated the condition. ("Perpetuated" is an understatement, considering that eons have passed.)

This may seem utterly fantastic and mind-boggling, yet if we think of the allegory of Adam and Eve, we see this illustrated in a way that most of us have heard since childhood. Adam and Eve lived in Paradise, or in Oneness, in harmony with the Divine Principle. They ate, or accepted into consciousness, the fruit of the Tree of the Knowledge of Good and Evil, the knowledge of opposites rather than Oneness. Accepting opposites invites judgment. Living in Oneness supports diversity through acceptance.

The allegory teaches that God banished Adam and Eve from the Garden. This would be like saying that the principle of electricity punishes us if we misuse it. Having become conscious (eating the fruit) of both good and evil (opposites), Adam and Eve brought forth their own judgments. It is not that Adam and Eve left the Garden of Eden; it is only that their perceptions became imperfect; they saw opposites rather than diversity. We are told that Adam hid from God because he was naked. But it was Adam who judged himself naked, not God. God asked him, "Who told thee thou wast naked?" Before ingesting the knowledge of opposites, there was no way to judge nakedness or "clothed-ness." There was just "Beingness."

To return to that Edenic state of awareness, we must bring ourselves back to the *conscious* awareness of Oneness. We must understand that whenever or whomever we judge, we are really sentencing ourselves.

I am grateful for the memory of the experience uncovered with JD. Its impact on my life has been by far the deepest and the most difficult to put into practice because even though I know I must not judge, I must still exercise discernment. I must learn to look at situations that *appear* to be opposites, such as fair/unfair, healthy/sick, young/old, and not pass judgment on them. I must look beyond the appearance of things to an expanded spiritual perspective. How does that work?

If we are looking at a country in the midst of a civil war with all its destruction and atrocities of war, it is easy to call one side right and another wrong, one side cruel and another the victim. If we are to return to Oneness, we must adjust our perception. It is none of our business nor is it our right to pronounce one side right and one side wrong. Our business is to return to the awareness of Divine Principle.

At first I had to ask myself if we should ignore the wounded, the homeless, and the devastation. No. The answer must be that we do not. Neither do we make a judgment. We must do all that we can to ease suffering and diminish destruction. Offer aid, assistance, and shelter to those in need. Look to bring compromise, treaty, and understanding to those in conflict. Do all this in the awareness that the aggressor, the victim, you, me, and everyone are Divine Being. Each is having a divine spiritual experience no matter how it may appear. Perhaps they have forgotten their spiritual roots. To forget that we are Spirit Being does not take away our spirituality, it only makes us temporarily ignorant of who we really are. When we withhold judgment and act according to our *expanding awareness of truth*, we can and do stimulate that same awareness in others.

When we judge, when we perceive life as being only what our physical senses and rational mind present to us, we are sentencing ourselves to a life lived in limitation and separation.

Chapter 12

NIGHT SKY

Many months after the incident with JD, another piece of the puzzle presented itself. I was working at home when in the distance I heard a rhythmic sound. Because ceiling fans in some of the rooms occasionally make a clicking noise as they spin, I didn't give the sound much consideration. But it was late autumn and the fans were not running, so I stopped working to listen. Gradually the rhythm became a discernible chant: "I-O-A." I wondered what significance there could be in those vowels. I listened more intently and identified the pattern as "I-O-*PA*." The "P" was more like a "P-T" sound, with "A" emphasized. It was repeated several times, then word-like sounds were added without changing the cadence of the chant. Recognizing that this might be a prelude to another past life, I stopped work, sat down, and closed my eyes.

A figure lies face up on a large red-brown altar stone in a cave or perhaps a tomb. His face is painted with many bright colors, making it look like an exotic creature. The cheekbones are high and well-defined. The face itself is sexless. Even through the paint, there is an ageless quality about his features. His bare chest is painted with some brightly colored symbols. Several people are standing and moving about. I sense the person lying on the slab is me.

I then do something I have never done before in these meditations: I leave the chair and lie on the bed, flat on my back, covering my heart with my hands, one over the other. Almost immediately I feel a deep stabbing pain in my chest. At this point, something like static interferes and the experience ends. The pain in my chest vanishes.

I was curious. Such interference had never happened before, nor had I ever changed positions during an experience.

I felt an inexplicable affinity for the figure on the altar and I thought of him often, of how pure and beautiful he was. Had this been some kind of ritual sacrifice? But I had lain with hands crossed over my heart. This was the posture of the dead, not one about to be sacrificed. What was my connection with this event? Almost a year was to pass before more information presented itself.

One afternoon while reading the channeled works of Ascended Masters, I came across a passage from an American Indian Master. I tried skipping ahead to another section but for some reason I flipped back to the Indian Master's section, thinking I'd just skim those few pages.

As I read, I began to feel fidgety and unsettled. I wanted to put the book down, or at least skip that part, but somehow I couldn't. In the far reaches of my awareness, I heard a kind of chanting, but refused to listen or give it credence. Finally, I could sit still no longer. I was so resistant to reading further that I jumped up and began pacing back and forth. The pacing gradually changed into a kind of dance, not ballet or modern movement, but a deliberate action with its own grace and purpose, seeming to pick up, bend, and fold my body into its own shapes. I don't know how long this lasted, but it felt wonderful and very natural. Slowly the dance ended and the Indian Master began to speak to me. I sat cross-legged on the floor, eyes closed, listening.

I heard the hugeness of his humor and the warmth of his love as he asked, "Do you remember?"

"No," I answered.

"Remember the night sky? Think of the night sky," he urged.

I am on a flat hilltop, looking at the night sky. It is a spectacular indigo sea of endless color and possibilities. The fiery light of the stars blazes forth, begging to be touched. Each star is flawless and known to me. The constellations are living creatures in motion as I watch. The moon, huge and perfectly round, is a brilliant sun in a different kind of day. My eyes shift to the horizon. The night sky blends into the Earth like lovers in an embrace, two different spirits melting into a new and exquisite life. My heart opens with love for the Earth and the night sky.

The Master whispers, "Your name was Night Sky Kissing Earth. Remember our time together? What fun we had?" I hear and feel his humor. "What a good spirit-seer you were." His voice changes, becoming soft and comforting. "But you were too young...too young for your gifts. Remember?"

I now see a young man, one of the original people of that land. This is a vast land mass predating and encompassing most of what we know as the world today. I call him an Indian, but his appearance is much different from the Indians of North or South America. He looks like a mixture of ancient Egyptian, Mayan, and some other quality, a universal quality. There is something about his appearance that seems to embody both sexes and all races.

The young man's face is perfectly shaped and hairless, neither totally masculine nor totally feminine but rather androgynous. His features and body are exquisite. He sits alone and still on a hilltop. It is night. He loves looking into the night sky. He prefers the night to day, feeling more at ease in moonlight than sunlight. I feel a love for the young man and for some unknown reason, an abiding sympathy.

I hear the Indian Master speak: "You had much power. You could see through the night sky into the cosmos, into the past and into the future. You were also a gifted healer. From your presence, your look, one could receive. Do you remember?"

I whisper, "Yes, yes I do." I can remember, but there is a large part of me that does not want to. I am afraid to remember.

The Master speaks again: "Now, my old friend," he says with the tenderness of a father toward a newborn, "you must finish this. Look at the night sky."

I become one with the young Indian. I sit on the hilltop watching the night sky, feeling content and peaceful. This is "my ground." I have consecrated this hilltop and commune with the "Spirit of All" here. Gazing into the sky I see the future of what is known now as the Americas. I am engrossed in the saga that unfolds before me in the night sky.

As I stare into the indigo heavens, the history stops. The sky parts, as if it were only a painted curtain. I see "my home," the distant world I come from. I recognize it and know I am of that place, those beings. This awareness and recognition causes great pain and passionate longing as I realize I am not who or what I thought I was. Anguishing over my true "home" and "family," I take a knife and without care or thought, plunge it into my heart.

The experience ends. Abruptly I remember the chanting and the young man on a stone slab. I know it is Night Sky's burial ceremony. As Night Sky, I watch that ceremony, not fully understanding what has happened. I am free from my body but at the same time, not free.

The Indian Master begins to speak to me of grounding myself in the present moment. He instructs me to breathe deeply in steady breaths and to exhale easily through my mouth. As I concentrate on breathing with a comfortable rhythm, he tells me to straighten my back, lift my chin, and keep my hands loosely on top of my legs. I am sitting cross-legged on the floor as these instructions are given.

The Master advises me that the energies remaining from this experience must now be allowed to move through to their completion. He explains that mental, emotional, and physical shifts must take place. There is still much sadness, confusion, and grief remaining from that lifetime that can now be released through understanding and acceptance. Information from past experiences record themselves in "spiritual memory cells," he tells me. These cells are held in the heart center in each lifetime. At various points in our life, the Master explains, the cells are activated and pour their information into our nervous system. When the "memory cells" are activated in a person who is not living an aware existence, he or she will react to energetic impulses in the nervous system without knowing why or what has caused a particular behavior. If we are living a spiritually aware life, we may recognize when this activation occurs. Once we are conscious that the cells are active, we may set about neutralizing them.

This is not as daunting a task as imagined. The Master explains that what needs to be done is to accept the energy from the *past* experience and transmute it into energy for the *present* life. The point is to clear the past energy of its pain and fear so that it once again becomes pure life energy and can be used to further one's path toward spiritual awakening.

In silence, I balance my breathing and let the explanations of the Master rest in my mind. After I have found a rhythm and ease in breathing and feel fully alert to my surroundings, the Master begins to speak again. He talks with the ease and comfort of an old friend, reminding me of the things we used to do together. He speaks not so much to distract me from the feelings of the Night Sky experience but more to walk me through the phases of remembering, allowing, and integrating these feelings. He tells how we would project an emotion (ours or someone of the community who asked us for help), such as fear, sadness, or anger, into a particular species of animal.

There were all types of birds and animals living on the land mass such as large cats, deer, large ox-type animals, and a great variety of birds. He explains how we would sit quietly, conjure up the emotion, and hold it until we reached a kind of trance-like state. We would then ask an animal to enter into our awareness or trance. When we felt the animal's presence, we would empty all that particular emotion into it through a kind of thought-feeling. In a matter of days or sometimes only hours, an animal of that species would present itself to us as an offering. We would give thanks to the willing animal-being for taking our emotion, ingesting it, and making it its own. In so doing, the animal was able to empower the species by transmuting the accepted emotion into a higher energy.

We and the community would then ceremoniously slay and eat the animal. Ingesting the animal's flesh would, in turn, empower us by returning to us the energy of our emotion now purified as gratitude. It required both extreme concentration and purity of motive to transfer and transmute emotional energy. This ability was the greatest service performed by the spirit-seers for the community. Animals were not hunted by people or other animals for food but eaten only when an animal offered itself. Such was the relationship between animals and humans at that time. Animals and man lived in harmony to celebrate the living Earth. Life and death were looked upon as ways to revere the planet.

The Master spoke warmly of how long we had known each other almost from the beginning. This Indian Master is the Old Man in the experience with JD. In the eons between then and now, the Old Man had attained Masterhood. Gratefully he was here to help me remember and to encourage me to master myself.

Chapter 13

GIFTS FROM NIGHT SKY

This experience was much different from the others, making it unusual to analyze. My invisible teachers had never interacted with me as fully as the Indian Master. Such communion enabled me to integrate that lifetime more efficiently and faster, although it will be years before I can truly understand and apply that wisdom.

For months, thoughts of Night Sky brought tremendous sadness and heart-wrenching sympathy. Gradually I began to understand that having sympathy for Night Sky was a way of keeping myself separate from him and the experience. As long as I was sympathetic, I was not allowing my *self* to respond to the deeper issues of that lifetime. As the sympathy and sadness for this experience dwindled, a ripening process occurred that was hard to explain. It felt like confidence but without the personal investment. It was similar to fearlessness but with a sense of grand anticipation.

When I became "one" with Night Sky, I felt the enormity of his inner power, but it was an unpolished, innate power. Because he hadn't consciously developed it himself, Night Sky did not understand or honor its potential.

At birth, Night Sky had been recognized as a spirit-seer and was given to be raised by all the members of the community, having no one mother or father from the moment of his birth. It was considered an honor for parents to offer their child as a healing gift to the community. From a very young age, Night Sky would keep himself awake at night so that he could watch the stars. He grew to know and love each star and in his boyish heart dreamed of living in the night heavens. He felt as if he were a sea creature and the night sky the ocean in which he found life and nourishment. When he became older, he was accepted into the inner circle of thirteen spirit-seers. While this brought him contentment, he never surrendered his love for the night.

He considered his abilities as neither a burden nor a benefit. He cared for the community, yet in his heart he remained detached from everyone except the Sun Searcher, the seer responsible for the community's total well-being, a role that could be filled by a male or female. All spirit-seers were identified at birth by signs in the heavens and on Earth. Although he was much older, the Sun Searcher was Night Sky's closest friend. It had been the Sun Searcher's intention to gradually develop in Night Sky an appreciation for his gifts, but the community was growing rapidly and time did not allow such a process. The people were becoming less tolerant of one another, with emotional disruptions and increased quarreling. This put heavy demands on the spirit-seers. Night Sky and his gifts were needed constantly; there was no time for instilling appreciation.

Night Sky showed me that although we may desire to come into the full awareness of our gifts and power, most of us have no idea of the magnitude of those aspects of Self. To be the fullness of our Spirit Self is to know and understand these gifts and their power. To have these abilities and power without the spiritual understanding may hinder our life rather than help it, as though we are a rare and luscious fruit that, when ripe, will offer sweetness, delicacy, and variety. All our potential is there but must ripen to reach its fullness. So, too, our spiritual understanding must have time to mature. Maturity ensures that our gifts of Spirit will be applied for the benefit of ourselves and for all life. Night Sky's experience highlighted for me the need for patience. I understood that everything has its own season and will come to fruition in a natural and comfortable way—*if we do not interfere.* All that is required of us is to live consciously, knowing we are Spirit Being. Our soul will do the rest.

If Night Sky had had a depth of spiritual understanding, he would not have acted so hastily. Because he did not recognize his abilities as qualities of Spirit Self, he did not respect the opportunity life offered him. He was barely seventeen when he died. The gifts of his spirit were pressed into service before they could be rooted in maturity and gratitude.

From other past experiences, but especially this one, I realized that gratitude was an important component in bringing spiritual awareness into human experience. It is not gratitude to *anyone*, it is gratitude for Life and Its diversity.

I believe that today's practice of eating animals actually stems from that prehistoric wizardry of transmuting emotional energy as described by the Indian Master. I feel that animals still can and want to serve humanity as converters of our base emotions. It seems to me that the opposite of this conversion takes place when we slaughter animals in fear and without reverence for their lives. When we eat their flesh under those circumstances, are we not ingesting the animals' fears and pain?

I have spent many hours with the Indian Master since this experience. He has communicated volumes of information on the function of the "spiritual memory cells." Basically, the cells contain memories of emotional, mental, and physical events— positive as well as negative. The positive energy is often held in reserve as a balancing quality until the negative charge is released and purified. Then the positive charge releases in a way that we can understand and use. This means that as the energy is purified, we come into a greater range of abilities and inner power. If we are living a spiritually unaware life when these cells activate, at worst we experience this release as confusion, disorientation, schizophrenia, and phobias. At best, we ignore or squander an opportunity to achieve greatness of Spirit.

One final comment regarding Night Sky: Here, too, judgment had played a part. When the heavens parted and he saw his "home," he judged his Earth existence as meaningless and less worthy than his remembered "home." Perhaps if he had been older, more mature, he might not have acted in such haste. Had he allowed his vision to continue, he may have seen himself and the Sun Searcher in that other experience of eons ago. Would he have recognized the Sun Searcher as the Old Man? If so, he could possibly have understood how he came to be separated from his "home." If only he hadn't been so quick to pass judgment.

Chapter 14

SUMMARY AND REFLECTIONS

Y
ou may think all the experiences I have related are about suffering, pain, and loss. Actually, the opposite is true. They are about joy, freedom, and attainment. They reflect the mutable nature of our perceptions and beliefs and how these influence our lives. My experiences confirmed that the more accurately our perceptions and beliefs conform to Spiritual Reality, the greater freedom we each have. The term Spiritual Reality is difficult to define but I consider it to be that which is eternally true, that which is not subject to personal perception, and that which does not change (even though our perceptions of It do).

From these experiences I *know* that Life, that individual Being, is eternal. This individual Being or Soul may have many distinct forms and scores of different experiences, but It will always be the *same essence of Self*. It is as if our *Self* (the Spirit essence of each individual) is a cosmic movie actor playing many unique characters set in different locations and at various periods of history—but we are the *same essence or being* throughout each role.

It may be that as we watch our image on the movie screen we are startled. We had no idea how we looked in our makeup and costume. If we are not paying attention, we might even think it isn't us. We are still our Selves, no matter how flawed or flawless the makeup and costume. We have died hundreds of times in our various roles, yet we continuously return to perform in a new drama, each new part offering opportunities to develop our skill.

As performers, we would not call our co-actors "wicked" simply because they portrayed murderers, prostitutes, or thieves. We know it was not them, only the characters they chose to portray.

The next part might require playing a saint. Saint or sinner, underneath the layers of paint and costume, they are still Themselves. So it is with human beings. Underneath the facade of material form and intellect, we are still our Selves, Spirit Being in essence, human being for the experience, be it tragedy, comedy, or melodrama.

These lifetimes revealed to me that the only time I can possibly make a right and just judgment is when I can rise above what my physical senses and intellect present to me and see what is happening spiritually. What is occurring in the spiritual realm must always comply with spiritual law. Regardless of how things may look to my human perception, spiritually, all is in order. The only possible judgment that spiritual perception can make is, "There is nothing to judge." What may appear as lack, disease, or death on the "movie screen of life" is really an *opportunity* for various actors (Spirit) to learn, develop, and mature in their skills. Each lifetime is an occasion for a particular type of learning, entered into with agreement by all concerned. The players act out their tragedy or comedy and incorporate what has been learned into their repertoire. Then, it's on to the next life, very much the attitude of the Crusader.

The greatest gift from these experiences was a clearer picture of human dynamics and how our judgments create our life experience. This is an impersonal, creative process which shows us in a tangible way what is hidden in our consciousness. If we notice how, where, when, and why we pass a judgment, we can begin to see what beliefs we have assimilated that are not compatible with our Divine nature.

The most powerful theme in every experience is judgment and its effect upon the object of judgment, but most powerfully upon ourselves. When we are told to "judge not lest ye be so judged," it seems a logical and somewhat neutral statement but from my own experience, I have learned to respect it and to see in it a ticket to spiritual awareness and human freedom. Judgment is a mirror reflecting back to us what is in *our* own consciousness. Whatever judgment we make must already exist in our *own* consciousness, otherwise we would not be aware of such a condition.

For example, if you were to judge someone greedy, you must have in your own consciousness the awareness of greed or how else would you recognize it? Does that mean that you are greedy? Perhaps, but more to the point, it means that you are focusing on a *perception* and then fastening that perception onto a person. Consider this: Greed can not exist in a consciousness that is aware of Itself as Spirit. Such a Consciousness *knows* that Its every need will be met, and abundantly so, from within its own Self. Spirit has no need to look outside Itself, or to hoard. How does spiritual Consciousness view greed? Awakened Consciousness would regard greed the same as it would disease, "sin," or death—as *ignorance* of one's True identity. Why call a person greedy, sick, malicious, or criminal, when their only failing is temporary amnesia, forgetting that they are Spirit Being? When you realize that every need you or anyone can ever imagine is taken care of before it becomes a need, you will no longer lack, or judge anyone or anything. You may recognize when others are operating in ignorance of their True Identity, but this will elicit compassion, not judgment.

Any pain or suffering incurred by the character in each life-. time remembered occurred because they passed judgment and whether it was self-judging or the judging of another or a circumstance, the consequences were the same: a *sense* of loss of freedom, loss of love, and loss of life. I use the word "sense" because each experience proved to me that whatever was suffered by each person was due only to their *perception*, to their limited sense of themselves and their world. *This perception did not alter their Divine Identity.*

The French Woman judged herself and all others so harshly that she could find no place in heart or mind for forgiveness. Her perception that she could not face her family or forgive her husband kept her a prisoner of her own inflexibility and finally ended her life.

The Child in the monastery suffered because of her belief in a punishing and unforgiving God. She saw herself as a sinner and passed her own judgment, a sentence so severe as to extinguish all hope.

The Crusader found himself in a war he didn't believe in. He did not trust his own knowing and perceived another as having the answers for him. He judged himself incapable of knowing what he felt in his heart was true.

The most powerful and exacting consequence of passing judgment was in the fourth experience related to JD. Pure Consciousness became tainted by allowing a perception to distort the Truth. Once the judgment was issued, a clouded image of reality shackled the soul to the human arena.

When Night Sky saw his true "home," he acted with deliberate haste, judging that he could not be happy in a world so different from his remembered "home." He forfeited the opportunity to express his spiritual gifts.

No matter how much pain or anguish was experienced in each lifetime, Truth demonstrated that Consciousness is ongoing, unlimited, and perfect. It is our limited *sense* or *perception* that causes and perpetuates a life lived in restriction and fragmentation. When we can rise above our human senses and push back the borders of limited thinking, then our perceptions will begin to conform more closely to spiritual Truth. Once consciousness is expanded to take a higher view of life, a view that extends beyond the physical senses and intellect, beyond our sense of time and space, then life begins to function in an orderly, compassionate, and loving manner.

With each memory I had to ask myself, "What is the lesson here?" It was not enough to simply receive a revelation; there had to be a purpose for it. I've come to accept that a major purpose was to gather up pieces of my Self (soul). Through ignorance and forgetfulness, I had imagined I was a self separate and apart from my God. Now those separate parts are coming together.

Can something Divinely perfect be separated? Of course not! Yet, if we regard ourselves and our world exclusively through our five physical senses, we begin to believe we *are* separate from our God Self, that we are only an ego or personal self—i, me, my, mine. We will define ourselves as *my* body, *my* mind, *my* feelings. If we do not remember we are Spirit, we will assume our human perception is the only truth, resulting in a life where we see ourselves, other people, the planet, animals, and plants as disconnected pieces. We then forget we ever had a memory of spiritual Oneness and slip deeper into unconsciousness. We will stay in this coma until something prompts us to remember. One purpose of these revelations was to pull together those fragmented misconceptions of Self and to remember something that *we all know* but may have forgotten—*our Wholeness.*

Gratefully, I do remember this feeling of being whole. I felt it when I was before the tribunal, begging to come in, and in that fluid crystal form as I watched Man walking upon the Earth. And, of course, that state of completeness was felt in the moment that I recognized my God.

The reason for any revelation is to awaken memories of True Identity, and once remembered, to live accordingly. Certainly every sentence, every word in these revelations and memories had profound significance for me. Learning that *each of us* springs from God to *become* God, and that there are as many Gods as there are individual Beings, was profoundly different from anything to which I had ever been exposed. And to shift my consciousness to a more expanded level, total surrender of my beliefs was required.

It was evident that to linger in a belief, even a good or comfortable one, is contrary to spiritual growth. If we wish to ride the high seas of eternity, we must be willing to lose sight of the shore. To sail uncharted oceans requires the desire and the courage to go beyond our own narrow perceptions, to embark upon the unknown waters of spiritual exploration, to trust.

What we are trusting is our *inner* Self, our Soul, that place deep within us where we *know*, where we intuitively feel there is an invisible world of spiritual Oneness, harmony, and immortality. Once we feel or recognize the Self, we must be willing to relinquish all beliefs that *no longer serve* our expanding awareness, to discard all for Allness. This surrender is an ongoing process. It is trusting that your heart's intention to know the Truth will keep you from any major folly.

These revelations brought with them an understanding of what human beings see as life is not, in fact, Life. It is an experience. WE ARE LIFE. WE ARE ONGOING, ETERNAL LIFE. What we consider to be our everyday existence is but a moment of experience for the Soul. It is fleeting, with no permanence, imperfect, finite. Real Life is God-Life and must therefore be of the substance or essence of God—*which we know we are*—when we are *not* being mis-informed by our perceptions.

In today's fast-paced world, we travel in supersonic jets, eat microwave meals, drink instant coffee, and receive world news as it happens. Life's convenience and quick reactions have created an environment that is noisy, active, and demanding. We often find ourselves swept along by this tide of commotion. It is so easy to forget in this rapid-fire world that we are Divine Children of Divine Creation. And as Divine Children we have at any moment and at every moment the ability to choose between being caught up in the outer world or electing to take time to rest into the inner world.

All the things we seek in the outer world—power, abundance, peace, recognition, well-being—are already a part of our makeup and available to us within the solace of our own Soul. This is because there is only *one* Substance (that which emanates and originates from the One Creative Principle). All life is formed of this Substance, and since this Substance is formed from the Creative Principle, It *must* be everything the Creative Principle is.

For example, we may look at a desk made of oak. The desk has all the qualities of oak inherent in it. It may look and act as a desk, but its substance is oak. We cannot take the "oakness" out of the desk just because it looks like a desk and not like an oak tree. So it is with us. We may look, act, and even believe that we are physical human beings, but our essence, our nature, is Divine Substance. We cannot be separated from our Divinity.

In accepting a gift of revelation, we also accept the responsibility to incorporate what is learned and revealed into the daily business of living, whether we are cleaning house or governing a nation; they are all the same to our soul. We must *live* our Truth. Any spiritual teaching or revelation will only remain inspiration if we do not incorporate it into our daily life. The purpose, value, and responsibility of revelation is what makes an experience a *revealing*. The purpose is to expand consciousness, to reveal "new worlds," "new truths," "new Gods." I hope this expansion will continue into infinity and through eternity for me and for you. The only reason why such expansion would ever cease is if we choose to hold unshakably to our beliefs and our limitations.

The value of Truth revealed is its ability to bring heaven to Earth; that is, to alter the way we relate to each other and our environment. Before, we may have thought that we had to compete, maneuver, or outsmart one another for success or to earn a living. Thanks to Truth revealed, we see things differently. We recognize cooperation and divine service as the source of our success and the fountain of our wealth. We begin to work, not for a living, but for the simple joy of expressing the individual qualities of our Soul. As we do that, we are able to recognize those soul qualities in others as well.

Stop reading for a moment and visualize your home, your office, and your community functioning through compassion, understanding, and cooperation rather than through fear, competition, and selfishness. Can you see *yourself* as the catalyst for change in your environment? You can bring about these changes *in proportion to the expansion of your own individual awareness.*

The task intrinsic in revelation is for us to begin to live this new vision. How? We may begin by adjusting our behavior to comply with our understanding and by developing habits that support our vision. This can seem overwhelming at first, but it doesn't have to be done all at once. We can ease into new behavior a little at a time. I have learned to start with simple changes.

For example, as I began to understand the connectedness of all things, the Earth and its welfare became important to me. Truth revealed showed me that how I treat anyone or anything in my life is how I treat my Self or God. Therefore, any act of irreverence against Man, animal, or the planet is detrimental to my *own* well-being.

I live in a community that has limited curb-side recycling, so for those things not picked up by the town, I personally would have to take quite a distance from my home in order to recycle them. I didn't want to be bothered with that added effort and responsibility. For a while, I would recycle some things and throw others in the regular trash. As my consciousness expanded, it became harder not to make the extra effort to recycle everything no matter how far I had to travel. This may sound insignificant, but such a commitment establishes Truth in and as your very own consciousness.

I knew Truth was firmly installing itself when once I had to reluctantly dig through the trash compactor for a plastic container. I had thrown it away because I didn't feel like going to the trouble of recycling it. I thought, "This is ridiculous. Why am I looking through this mess for a single plastic carton?" Grumble, grumble. I found it, washed it, and set it aside to start another pile of things to be taken to the recycle location. At that moment, I knew Oneness had become so much a part of my consciousness that I could only act in accord with It—otherwise, I would be in conflict with myself.

Recycling is a little thing but the motivation behind it is an infinite thing, a way to honor what I recognize as Oneness. The purpose is always to make Truth real for you, to realize your

Oneness. It must become so much a part of you that you are no longer aware of it as a Truth, but it is simply who you are.

I believe there is enough Spiritual Truth known and available to the world today to make this planet a paradise, so why isn't it? If we look at the world's religions, it is easy to see that spiritual knowledge is a part of each religious creed.

Most religions have at least one person who has exemplified the spiritual truth of that faith—Buddha, Mohammed, Jesus, Krishna to name a few. Each of these souls lived a life of sublime example. We, for the most part, have taken their exemplary lives and ignored the *model* they provide for us. We end up worshipping the signpost rather than following its direction. Rather than seeing these souls as a standard to achieve for ourselves, we have made these great way-showers into idols and lost sight of the ideal they represent. Neither you nor I can aspire to be an idol. An idol has no life to sustain it; it is an empty effigy. However, anyone who has held to an ideal has reached their mark to some degree.

We can search inwardly for our spiritual ideal and come to recognize what we value as that model, be it a life lived as Jesus, Buddha, Mohammed, or our own concept of a Divine Principle. Then if we adjust our everyday actions to conform to that model, our world will reflect that ideal.

It is as simple as this: What you hold dear, what you value, what you turn your mind to, is what your life will become. If you turn your mind to acquisition, if you love money and things, that becomes your ideal, and in greater or lesser measure that is what your life reflects—a life governed by money, where your happiness, peace of mind, daily activity, and how you treat people depends on your financial state. Imagine instead that your life is governed by a spiritual ideal in which your happiness, peace, and attitude depends on the degree of love, forgiveness, and service you show. Which life would express more freedom? Which life would create a heaven on Earth?

Of all that has been imparted to me, I think how wondrous it is, how much hope and promise each expression of Truth brings to us all. Can you sense this? Can you see how important you, the individual, are to both humanity and the realms of Spirit?

I know it is easy to forget we are Spiritual Beings, especially when we are first awakening to Truth. Yet you do not have to learn anything, or strive for anything, or become anything. You only need to *remember* the Truth about yourself and all life, that *We are all Divine Souls of Divine Creation with the same nature and characteristics of that Creation. Allness is your identity.* If you can remember what that means, if you can remember what it feels like to be connected to all things (and you can if you give yourself the chance), could you possibly need anything? Could you maliciously destroy, hurt, or in any way damage anything? So what do you think? Do we need more food in the world, more money, more peace, more property? Or do we need, *more than anything else*, to *remember*, to *recognize*, and to *honor* the One Life individually expressed as you, as me, as friend, as foe?

It is now many months since I started writing this book and in all the thinking, meditating, and writing, I have come to a deeper understanding of not only life in general, but of humanity. In the beginning, not only did I not understand my fellow humans I didn't particularly like them. I lived just to get through this life as fast as possible, to be free from this human experience and return to my "home." But now I have come to appreciate my human experience and my place in it. After all I have written and thought about ONENESS, I now feel for the first time at peace and at one with humanity. At this point, I wish to express my gratitude to you, Dear Reader.

If there had been no hope of a reader, I probably would not have written this. And if I had not written, then I would not have come to this point of understanding.

I have always loved animals and plants because I saw them as loving unconditionally. They don't judge, measure, or compare us; they simply accept us. I didn't feel that way about mankind. I saw humanity as judgmental, unforgiving, and egotistical. As I worked on this book, I came to a realization: It is not *humanity* that manifests these characteristics; it is, and always has been, *me* and *my perceptions. I* was the one who judged. *I* was the one unwilling to forgive. *I* was the one who lived a "me, my, mine" existence. Humanity is perfect, going about its chosen path of learning, growing through experiencing duality by feeling separate from its God-Self. It is a fine way to learn. The fact that humanity didn't measure up to my expectations did not make it good or bad, only different.

I wrote this book to say that we all have a free and eternal Life. That Life is happening right *now*, right *here* and you don't have to die to experience it. This is not meant to be a "how to" book but more of a remember-who-you-are book. Do my shared experiences feel familiar to you? Can you feel something tugging at your heart or in your mind that feels like a distant memory? Because we are each individual, we will not have the same experiences or interpret them alike. I did not relate this adventure so that you may travel the same road as I, only that you may *desire to take your own inner journey and discover your own truth.*

Do be patient with yourself and your chosen path. And remember, you are eternal Being, so there is no hurry. Relax. Consider how long eternity is.

SECTION III

*Do not be afraid to question everything and everyone
in your spiritual search.
The Truth will remain the Truth
no matter how often you question it.
An awakening person manifesting Spirit remains constant,
Loving you without condition
Allowing your experiences without judgment
Understanding your questioning and your quest,
For they have "been there, done that."*

QUESTIONS AND ANSWERS

Regarding Personal Living

How can I develop spiritual awareness when I have a family and obligations to deal with daily?

Try to set aside ten, fifteen, or twenty minutes each day to read spiritual material or simply to be quiet. Learn to meditate. Take a class or a weekend workshop. Or select one aspect of your life that you feel does not express spiritual qualities; for example, gossiping. Simply by making a conscious commitment to yourself not to participate in rumor-spreading or talking behind someone's back, you have taken the first step to develop spiritual awareness. It is not merely the act itself that stimulates the spirit within, *it is your **intention** to live a life of spiritual recognition*. That one *intent* opens the door to greater opportunities of Spirit.

Let's say you're ten pounds overweight, your high school reunion is in six months and you want to get back in shape before you see your old classmates. You have plenty of time and your goal is workable. How would you prioritize your time and energy? Would your obligations suffer because you are dieting? Would your family be neglected because you are getting in shape? Of course, you would need to be more diligent about certain aspects of your life, but nothing impossible or too disruptive. The hardest part would be to commit to your goal. So to answer your question with a question: *What are your priorities?*

Living a spiritually aware life *does* require a commitment from you. Just like dieting, you set reasonable parameters for yourself and take one step at a time. However, unlike dieting, once you've developed spiritual awareness, you can't slip backward. That awareness is yours forever, and the rewards far outweigh (no pun intended) any discipline or dedication required.

If I accept even part of what you say as true, how can I remain in my church?

Everything in this book encourages our spiritual nature and our connection with life. Does your church support this? If it does, there's no problem. Nothing in this book endorses elitism, intolerance, or judgment. Communing with friends and neighbors for the purpose of celebrating the God Within is the function of a church. If your church does this, then there is no conflict with accepting what is offered in this book, so attend your church. Do not be afraid to adjust your perception of your church to include a patient and compassionate allowance for doctrine. If you are happy with your church, stay. If you feel it doesn't support you at this time and place in your journey, take a leave of absence.

My partner is not on a spiritual path and it makes it hard for me to relate to him. What do you suggest?

Whether we know it or not, we are all on a spiritual path. Our inner journey is a very personal experience. No two people travel the same road at the same speed. No one can determine where another is on this journey. It could very well be that your partner is unconsciously behaving as though he is not interested in spirituality in order to prompt you to grow into your own knowing. He could easily be waiting for you to catch up to him. Do not judge whether he is or isn't on a spiritual path. Just honor your own search.

Any relationship can flourish if there is mutual respect and an atmosphere of *allowing*, of tolerance without judgment. Be grateful that you are conscious of your own true nature rather than trying to impart your spiritual perceptions. Remember, as you live *your* truth, you will awaken in others *their* truth.

My husband is not comfortable talking about spiritual practices or experiences that might exist outside of his traditional beliefs. So, we don't discuss it. Yet he supports my path by accommodating it. He never interrupts my meditation. He is patient when I have an experience that requires periods of quiet and stillness. He doesn't question me when I act from my spiritual knowing, even though from a human perspective such action doesn't make sense. It may *appear* that my husband is not on a spiritual path, but his acceptance and willing support of my journey shows that he is.

There must be other things you can share with your partner that will satisfy your sense of connection. Enjoy him for the gifts he brings to your relationship, like compromise, cooperation, tenderness, and playfulness.

This spiritual awakening business seems so complicated. Is there a shortcut?

Yes. Just *remember* your True Identity:
* Love without conditions or fear.
* Be compassionate with everyone, for chances are *you* have acted, thought, or behaved the same way at sometime in *your* journey, if not in this life, then in some other.
* Do not compare yourself with others or others with you.
* Embrace *all* experiences without judgment.

If everything I seek is already in my consciousness, already available to me, how can I bring things like prosperity, a new job, and a relationship into my life now?

Remember that your beliefs create your experience. If you want a more abundant, more interesting, more loving experience, *change your beliefs*. Beliefs about what, you may ask.

Do you believe any of the following to be true?
* You'll never get anywhere without the proper education.
* You've never had good timing, even when you were a child.
* You can't dance if you don't pay the piper.
* You can't teach an old dog new tricks.

- It doesn't take much to make me happy.
- You can't have it all.
- I could never do that.
- Life's a bitch and then you die.

The list is endless. Set aside one hour and write down some of your most significant beliefs. Now for the difficult part. Ask each belief whether it is Truth or just your *perception* of what is true.

Think of how you have made choices based on those beliefs. Remember, NOW is the only time there is, so forget the past and don't think of the future. Now find the place within yourself that lets you KNOW *you are Spirit Being, not just human being. And as such, all that divine Creation is, YOU ARE.* Start living that way. Begin by making choices *now* that reflect your developing belief in your spiritual roots. The choices you make *now* will be the *future* you will experience.

Will you explain what you mean by having an ideal and how to focus on it?

An ideal is a measuring stick. You focus on that ideal by *adjusting your behavior to comply with that objective.* Start acting the way you imagine you want to be and then you'll become it. This is putting into *practice* your desire to live a spiritual life.

Suppose you want to travel from Boston to San Diego (from human living to spiritual being). If you don't know where San Diego is, how are you going to get there? You can stumble around and possibly arrive by trial and error, but it would be simpler and more direct to get a map, see where San Diego is, and then set out on your journey. If you are in a hurry, you will focus on your destination and make choices that would take you directly toward the West Coast. If you were casual about your arrival, you might take side trips to see the sights and periodically check to see where you are in relation to San Diego. Whether you travel with deliberate intent or saunter, knowing where you want to eventually arrive will permit you to make the appropriate choices. Similarly, having a spiritual ideal keeps you on course.

Many men and women have exemplified spiritual living. For example, if you resonate with what Gandhi stood for, you might consider his life an ideal worth emulating. So decide for yourself what your highest understanding of spirit is and begin to adjust your behavior to comply with it by *practicing* living that way. Focusing on an ideal can be as simple as developing the *habit* of going to your Spirit Self *first* and taking action *after* you have had a quiet moment with your true Self. Developing the habit of *listening* to your Self before you act could be your first ideal.

Is there some way I can tell if I am living my ideal?

I cannot say what you consider to be evidence. I can tell you how I know when I am living my ideal: Life becomes simple. My needs dwindle, choices become clearer, change occurs naturally and easily. Loving without fear or expectation is more the norm than the exception. People, circumstances, and situations become *inclusive*, each with a gift of learning to give me and to receive from me. To sum it up, when I live outside my ideal, I see myself here just to have a wonderful life; when I focus on my ideal, I know I am here because *Life* is wonderful.

You said every need we could imagine is taken care of before it becomes a need. That doesn't make sense to me.

The Creative Principle is infinite potential; it holds every conceivable idea, invention, and condition. Everything already exists in the Creative Principle and Its Substance. For us to fill a need for anything, all we need to do is tap into Creative Substance. It is the reverse of "Necessity is the mother of invention," which says that first we have to have a need, and then we invent the solution. In Truth, the opposite happens. *The solution existed before the need presented itself. The awareness of the need simply means you have already tapped into the solution, which waited in the infinite invisible to be expressed.* Once you become aware of a need, the solution is already a part of your consciousness. It will form itself in such a way and fashion that you can understand and use if you let it. The more aware you are of this being True, the faster it happens. Albert Einstein understood this. He said his theories were not his; he just took a nap and when he woke up, the answers to a problem would be there.

What do you mean when you say we are each our own Truth?

A more accurate way to express this would be to say that we each are our own *level of awareness* of Truth. Truth is Infinite Awareness and we are each awakening to that Awareness at our own rates. So what may be true for me at a particular stage of my awareness may not be true for you, or even me at a different stage of awareness.

Regarding Children

How can I help my children remember their spiritual roots?

There are many things parents can do to foster spiritual awareness in their children. I believe most children, especially those born in the nineties, do preserve some memory of pre-existence, and you can encourage them to value and retain these memories. Ask them what it felt like before they became your child. If they refer to a past-life experience (not necessarily calling it that but inferring it), encourage them to tell you about it. One reason children (as well as adults) don't remember their identity as Spirit is that we are not stimulated or encouraged to do so. Talking about life existing before birth and after death activates this awareness, especially in children.

Traditional child rearing begins by teaching them that the five physical senses are the extent of their world. Anything not seen, heard, felt, smelled, or tasted is considered not real but imaginary and therefore is not valuable. With such a message, obvious or subtle, children assume that their perceptions of Spirit Being and Reality are incorrect. They then give up their true sense of Self for a limited human identity. The sad irony here is that these kids must then spend most of their adult life looking for what they already had and unlearning what society has taught them so that they may simply *remember* what they knew in the first place.

Constantly remind your children that they already *know*. Nothing is beyond their knowing. When they study, it is not to learn something they do not already know but rather to bring them into an *attitude of receptivity* where they may tap into the Knowing already within them. This is true for all of us, you and me, as well as for our children. Of course, adults have more to "forget" in order to remember that we are all part of a vast ocean of awareness that is ours by Divine descent. Before we came into material form, we existed; after we leave this physical form, we will still exist. We are ongoing, infinite, All-Knowing BEING. Once we enter into a human experience, we are forced to act as if we do not know who we are and therefore have to be taught. But *because divine Being is omniscient and we are divine Being, what is there for us to be taught*? It only remains for us to guide our children to remember their true Self.

Teach them the value of peaceful moments. Sit with them in silence so they can remember what it's like to just BE. This need not be more than one or two minutes a day, but it should be without interruption—no TV, music, or phone.

Help them develop a reverence for all life, no matter how insignificant it might appear. Even an annoying insect is worthy of the life that animates it. If you cannot escort the bug out of your environment then at least, if you must destroy it, do so without violence or malice. Teach that *everything* is connected by an invisible thread of spirit. This thread unites all life into ONE. In human form, this is called humanity. In spirit form, it is called God. The feeling of union with all life on the planet is the same as Allness. It is what we all felt *before* we incarnated. Such a concept will be familiar to most young children.

Two more things are extremely helpful in awakening spiritual identity in children. The first is to teach them to be *conscious*. This is a skill. If developed early, it will result in an adult life lived in understanding and peace. There is always a moment in any situation when we can *choose* our response. Such a moment goes unnoticed by someone who is not actively aware. In the aware person, such a moment is the point of power. Its recognition and use make the difference between living life as a victim or living it as Conscious Spirit Being.

Conscious living is responsible living, but this has nothing to do with burden or obligation. *Responsibility means the ability to respond in a CONSCIOUS way to whatever is happening.* It is simply another way of asking yourself, "What action do I choose?" You cannot respond if you are not aware that there is something to respond to. The ability to respond is not so much about doing the "right" thing or the "wrong" thing. It is knowing that, "right" or "wrong," *you get to choose.* Try *not* to speak to children of choices in terms of consequences. *Choices are roads taken.*

Every conscious or unconscious choice we make constitutes a step traveled in the soul's journey. If we make a "bad" choice, the result isn't a consequence to our soul, but simply a bumpier journey. We could have taken a smoother or faster road (choice), but at the time we acted, the more strenuous road had more appeal. Our choice reflects where we were *at that time* in our awareness. If we are not even aware we have a choice, it only shows how unconscious we are. By teaching your kids to recognize the moment of choice in all situations, you are teaching them to live a conscious, responsible life. This awareness and ability to respond is an important ingredient in spiritual living and fosters ever-increasing awareness.

The other helpful thing in awakening spiritual consciousness in your children is to avoid encumbering them with all the limitations of a human lineage, that is, do not pass on to your children your or your family's good or bad human qualities. Just keep reminding your kids of *their* spiritual qualities. Remember, each child born is a child of Divine Creation, not a child of Bill and Mary. Bill and Mary agreed to create the vehicle for a soul to enter into human experience, but recognize that that soul is *not just beginning life* when it is born. That soul *is life eternal.* It was life before it was born into human form and it will continue to be life after it leaves human form behind. Do not clutter that soul's experience with erroneous beliefs. Do not tell your children, "Oh, you must be careful about eating too much because all the women in our family have a tendency to put on weight." When you tell open, trusting children that they will get fat if they eat too much, they will believe you. Then that belief (which is really yours) becomes their reality. How do you know that being fat was one of the genetic characteristics that soul was planning to explore? If it was not, you have entered that limitation into your child's experience by stating as fact something that is really your belief about reality. Such statements, good or bad, are contrary to any child's spiritual heritage.

Can you remember when you were a child and expressed a talent for the first time? For example, the first time you drew a picture, you saw it as beautiful. In your child-innocence, you knew that the drawing came from your own Essence. You felt your talent. Children *know* they are talented, beautiful, and they have their own intelligence. This knowing does not come from a place of comparisons but from a place of *Oneness. Until the outer world begins to judge a child's appearance, IQ, or abilities, that child sees, senses, and trusts that he or she is perfect.* Children will blossom in their Knowing if we do not diminish or destroy it.

As most of us know, this Knowing can be destroyed by criticism and neglect. But have you considered how a well-meaning remark can set children to doubt their perfection? When you tell children that their beauty, talent, or intelligence comes from their uncle, mother, or father, you are telling them that they themselves cannot take the credit for these qualities. As parents we forget that our children may still be very much in touch with their spirit nature (at least until they are eleven or twelve years old). They still have a memory of their Completeness—a state of being where they feel the perfection of Self. Because they are physically and emotionally dependent on you, they can and will discard their inner knowing of Self for what you tell them. If you tell them they have talent because they inherited it from a relative, a child may translate that as, "This is not my own Being expressing Itself. This is something outside of Self given to me by my uncle." In a stroke, they are thus denied the vast repertoire of skills, talents, and wisdom from their spirit. It may take them a lifetime to recover these treasures, if ever. Our children come to us knowing and believing they have all that God has—all talent, all ability, all beauty, and all intelligence. You love and are concerned about your children, but try not to define *their* new life experience according to your own limited ideas.

What about heredity? Does it count?

Yes, of course, it is a factor. The soul *chooses* its parents partly for their genetics. But while the genetic pattern is an integral part of a soul's physical experience, it is *never* the Truth about the soul. The Truth is always perfection. If we remind and encourage our children to remember their spiritual identity, then any genetic condition can and will be met with grace and ease. If your child has the same talent as Uncle Henry (such as musical ability) then instead of saying, "You got that talent from your uncle," say, "It's great; you and Uncle Henry have the same talent."

That way, children's integrity is left intact and they don't have to surrender a part of their Knowing.

Are you saying we should let our kids walk around thinking they know everything?

No, but neither should they walk around thinking their abilities are defined by the size of their brain, the shape of their bodies, or the judgment of a talent scout or teacher. The knowledge, talent, or physical ability of children depends upon how much they recall of their spiritual nature. Reminding our kids that they come from a place of Knowing and that they only have to re-member develops an awareness and trust in their identity as Spirit Being.

Why don't all children have a "fairy person" to help them through the difficult times?

I don't know. I do know that all children (and adults) have access to Spirit. The invisible family and teachers who are a part of every soul's journey are always near their young earthly charges, but much may depend on the individual child's ability to respond to the invisible. The environment may also have some impact. If there are no quiet corners or alone moments, then it might be very difficult for a child to connect in a conscious way with his or her invisible help. But we must not forget, whether our children are consciously aware of it or not, that their spiritual family and teachers are ever-present, protecting, guiding, and loving them.

Regarding Trust

What do you mean by inner trust?

Webster defines the word trust as *confidence.* So to me inner trust means confidence in your individual perceptions of Self and God. These perceptions are how you know your God, how the invisible makes itself known to you, and how you interpret those events that are beyond words. These perceptions exist within your most private consciousness where no outsider can be privy to them. No one lives in your consciousness but you. For that reason, you alone must come to a point of acceptance regarding your experiences in spirit. You must recognize and trust that they have value and reality for you, even though these events cannot be seen, heard, touched, or rationally understood.

For me, developing an inner trust has been a slow and some-times difficult task. Probably for most true seekers, learning to trust spiritual guidance can be a strenuous and at the same time vital quality to acquire. Unfortunately, I do not have a quick, easy formula for developing inner trust.

Giving yourself permission to question anything and everything can take some of the stress out of the process. It's also helpful to ask Spirit to prove Itself to you or to support your faith in its existence until you can feel Its reality.

It's helpful to have people in your life who are also committed to spiritual awakening. This spiritual support system need be only one person, as long as he or she is open and encouraging. To surround yourself with people who think alike and strive for a knowledge of Truth does much to cultivate inner confidence. However, I recommend you keep to yourself whatever spiritual Truth you might receive until it has been incorporated into your consciousness. Try to avoid having to rely on your developing trust until it has actually taken root.

Why would you keep Truth to yourself? Isn't it true for everyone?

Yes, Truth is true for everyone, but not everyone interprets Truth the same way. We each are unfolding in our own manner, at our own rate. When you have an experience of the Truth, it is a sacred gift. It often takes time to digest its fullness. You have to "live" with this new vision of Spirit before it becomes a part of you. The gestation period is a tenuous time, and sharing an experience too soon, or with people who are not of your understanding or awareness, will dissipate its energy. By keeping silent, by holding sacred the spiritual gift you have received, it will become a permanent part of your consciousness.

You could sacrifice your spiritual experience and its gifts if you share them with those who are uninterested or unprepared. Criticism and intellectualizing can easily cause you to doubt and discard a gift from Spirit if you don't give it time to mature and explain itself fully in your consciousness.

And, of course, bragging or thinking that you are special because you received a revelation is also destructive. Remember, Spirit reveals itself to us so that we may expand our awareness to include *all* of life as God appearing AS. No one is more or less special in the eyes of Creation.

Why is trust so important?

Trust is what allows you to accept as real that which has no reality to the five human senses. Humanly, if you and others cannot see, hear, feel, or touch something, it is considered to be imagination. If the mind cannot account for an experience, it deems it inconsequential or even illusory. We would never know ourselves or others as a Spirit Being if we were to depend *solely on our intellect and five physical senses.*

Is trust the same as faith?

It may be. To me, the word *faith* implies trusting something *outside* of yourself, a faith *in* something, such as a God separate and apart from self. Trust seems more of an inner state. Call it faith or call it trust; it doesn't matter as long as it allows you to recognize and honor the God-Self that you are.

How do we develop trust in our invisible Self?

Slowly. Meditation and prayer speed the process along because in those quiet times you begin to remember what it feels like to *Know*. It may be fleeting, but *Knowing* is your true state, so you will recognize it. In time, you will begin to trust it.

For encouragement, read about other people's journeys and how they developed trust. Knowing that other people have succeeded in their spiritual search can ease you through periods of doubt and apprehension.

Look for the *synchronicity* in your life. When you think of an old friend and he or she calls you within minutes that tells that your needs are heard and are being met. Every time you recognize that the invisible hand of Spirit is supporting your spiritual search, say "Thank you." Your gratitude fosters a "friendship" with your inner Self which in turn cultivates trust.

Regarding Judgment

If judging is so detrimental to our spirit, what about judges passing judgment?

When judges impartially defend the laws of the land, they are simply doing their job. Judging becomes destructive when we fail to see that all life is God-Life regardless of how it may appear. People may *appear* as thieves or murderers, but their *real* identity is God Being appearing as human being. If we see only the human being with all its defects, that reflects what is in *our* consciousness. We are then destined to live in, as, and around those defects. Remember, *consciousness is what you are conscious of; what you are conscious of is your experience.*

Judges who maintain an impersonal attitude toward their work (not confusing the human behavior with the Spirit Being) are not passing judgment but only preserving the law. If a judge holds the inner awareness that all are Spirit Being having a human experience (not good or bad, only an experience), he or she will be doing significant world healing.

If we are not to judge, does that mean we are not to have opinions?

Can you have an opinion without comparing or judging? You may have a preference, a discerning awareness that prompts you move away from people, events, or things that are uncomfortable to you, or move toward those that are comfortable. Having preferences does not involve judging people or things as better or worse. All things are allowed their existence. Finding your place of ease does not require you to judge.

What is the difference between judging and discerning?

Inherent in judgment is the pairs of opposites. To have opposites you must have two (good/bad, right/wrong, old/young). In spiritual Consciousness there is only ONE. Things are neither good nor bad; they just ARE. They are not judged or compared. They are accepted as just Being.

Discernment is a learned skill. Before it is discernment, it is judgment. Through experience and spiritual awareness, judgment becomes less rigid and moves into opinion, where we are not so quick to condemn others, but we still compare. We think one person or situation is not as good, as beneficial, or as honest as ours. We say things like, "This is not a judgment, it's just my opinion," and then we proceed to pass judgment.

Through the process of developing spiritual preference, we connect with an aspect of Spirit that is *spiritual discernment.* Woven into this aspect is *intuition.* Our ability to spiritually discern usually begins as intuition. The sooner we begin to treat intuition as a valid and necessary component of spiritual life, the sooner we develop discernment.

Spiritual discernment is the ability to look at people, circumstances, and situations and *allow* them. That is, it allows Spirit to have any kind of experience it deems necessary, be it violent, sick, famous, or heroic. Spiritual discernment is seeing infinite, eternal Beings experiencing Themselves, each Being agreeing to help the other have the desired experience. This means that if a soul wishes to have the experience of being a savior, it will need someone to save, to agree to play victim in order for the other to play savior. Savior and victim are both equally eternal, infinite Beings. So what is there to judge? All are equal and are just having a different (but agreed upon) experience. Discernment allows us to see what is happening on the soul level.

This is *not* to say that we leave criminals on the streets, or continue to fight wars. It *is* to say that such conduct is only *behavior and not Being.* We can recognize that one person's scenario is not where we want to be. So we move on, leaving him to have his experience. If there is societal consensus that people displaying certain behavior be removed from the mainstream, we do that. But we do not label them good or bad—they are Spirit Beings having a human experience. The integrity of Spirit, yours as well as others, remains intact when we operate through discernment and not judgment.

I don't understand why anyone would want to be a victim.
First of all, you are assuming that being a victim is bad. Who are we to judge? From a higher perspective you can see that awaking consciousness can develop deep levels of compassion by experiencing powerlessness. Compassion allows the heart to open and release its love without conditions. It is well worth a lifetime or two as a victim if the soul learns to love through empathetic understanding.

The seemingly powerless victim is also in a place of enormous spiritual strength. If the victim is able to come to a state of true forgiveness toward the perpetrator and self, he or she ceases to be a victim. He or she becomes both the saved and the savior by recognizing that nothing could have taken place in his or her life unless agreed upon by all the souls involved. Such forgiveness *allows* Spirit its experience while not condoning the behavior.

Regarding Meditation

What do you mean by meditation?
It is an intent, an alert openness. The intent is to connect with your Divine Self. The alertness allows you to listen inwardly for confirmation of that connection. I think of meditation as a skill, one that can be learned. Once you know how to listen inwardly, you can meditate anywhere, at any time.

For me, meditation is *the moment of contact* with Self. It may last a fraction of a second or several minutes, but in that contact all human identity disappears. However, the *preparation* for meditation may take minutes or even hours before reaching that brief second of contact.

It is through the connection made in meditation that divine Being reveals Itself. This revealing is often so subtle that it may go unnoticed at first. In time, however, the effects and benefits of such contact will be unmistakable.

How do you still the mind's chatter?

It helps if you can quiet your outer surroundings. I think it is impossible to reach a state where the mind is blank, so don't try for that. Instead, begin by giving the mind something to consider or contemplate. Choose some spiritual passage that you'd like to understand better, or a situation where you wish to act with the highest spiritual integrity. Begin by stating your intention silently or aloud. For example, "I would like to see the deepest spiritual meaning in this experience." Then contemplate all the various ways it could be interpreted. In time, your mind will run out of things to ponder and you will experience a period, albeit brief, of stillness.

If I'm God, why do I have to sit and meditate?

Of course, you don't have to. But for most of us it is difficult to get our various awarenesses in alignment. Remember the example of having a headache, working your checkbook, and feeling anxious all at the same time? Each level on which we operate constitutes a level of our awareness. In order to connect clearly and consciously with our Spirit Self, these different levels must quiet down and come into an alignment.

Visually, I see each different level of awareness as a series of vertical grids. Imagine four grids: physical, emotional, mental, and spiritual. As we go about our daily lives, these grids swing from side to side, but not necessarily together. For example, physically, you may feel fine, so that grid is calm. Emotionally, you may feel irritated, causing the emotional grid to swing from side to side; depending on how irritated you are, the grid can swing gently or wildly. Mentally, you may be working through a dilemma, causing that grid to swing. Spiritually, your soul is waiting for the opportunity to flash its light through to you. In order for you to receive the fullness of your soul's light, the physical, emotional, and mental grids must be in alignment with each other. That is why we meditate. If you've found a way to align those grids without meditation, then by all means use it.

If you haven't found a way to align those levels of your awareness so that all are still and synchronized, it will be difficult for you to receive the full benefit of the soul's light. When we tap into our soul's guidance, it must flow through our mental, emotional, and physical bodies. The more aligned our levels of awareness, the more purely we receive the guidance.

Regarding Past Lives

Why can't I remember my past lives?

Why do you want to remember your past lives? This is not a flippant question but one worthy of your careful consideration and excruciating honesty, after which you can probably answer your own question.

One reason people don't remember their past lives is because the soul feels that such information at this time in its development would hinder rather than help. Let's say you are living a moral life, yet at the same time harboring rigid judgments about "good" people and "bad" people. If you were to spontaneously remember a lifetime as a brutal killer, such a shock might cause you to slip into harsh self-recrimination or abusive retribution, both of which could be detrimental to your present experience.

Not remembering past lives helps you focus on *this* life. Are your beliefs flexible enough for you to accept your past experiences without judgment?

Of course, the other reason we may not remember our past lives is simply that we haven't been taught to. Many children *do* remember their past existence, but by the time they grow to be seven or eight, they have been taught that such memories are imaginary and not valuable, so they forget.

How can I start to remember my past lives?

In general, most people can remember the past lives that are impacting their present existence. The qualities that the French Woman had locked in her heart were the traits I was meant to understand and transform in *this* life. That is why that lifetime was so near the surface of my consciousness.

There are books and people who specialize in helping others to remember past lives. Techniques like hypnosis and regression are also readily available and can certainly be useful if you are sure you wish to pursue them.

On your own, you can try meditating and asking your divine Self to reveal those lifetimes that are influencing your experience now. Be sure to keep a tape recorder or a pad and pencil handy and record all images and pieces of information you receive. Be patient and open, trust that your Self will give you what you most need to know—or not know.

Another technique involves remembering backwards. Start at the youngest age you can recall, then see if you can gently go back to an earlier time. Enlist your dreams to help you remember. Before going to sleep, place a pad and pencil by your bed. Write your intention on the top line of the pad. Make it clear and simple, such as "Memories of Important Lifetimes." Just before drifting off to sleep, remind yourself several times (some people say twenty-one times will ensure success) that you want information *and* that you will wake up and record the information once you receive it.

Of course, the easiest way to remember past lives is to *not forget* them in the first place. So, if you have children, encourage them to remember and value that continuity of identity. It would help if you could keep a record of their memories for them. When they are older they can use the information to bring to mind the issues they wish to explore.

How can I tell if I am remembering a past life or just imagining it?

It has been my experience that past-life information was charged with emotion and energy and always prompted genuine change in my life because it was a true memory.

The other quality always present in these experiences was a profound feeling of gratitude, a feeling we cannot fake, for it doesn't seem to come from our personality so much as from a pure place in the heart.

These are just my yardsticks; yours may be different. But what is certain is that if your intention is for soul growth, your soul *will* provide a way for you to know and trust your experience.

Keep in mind, however, that it is not the historical content surrounding a lifetime that is important. What is important are the soul lessons, so do not be concerned if you never receive a clear picture of a particular life. Examine the symbols used to present the material to you; they hold valuable information. Ask yourself what your feelings are surrounding this information and how it relates to your life now.

When you spoke of your father as the magician in the French Woman's lifetime, you said he chose to forget so much. What did you mean?

What we learn in each lifetime is never lost. This is because we are Spirit having a human experience and not the other way around. The human form may disintegrate, but the essence of the life experience is eternally recorded in the soul. It is always available to us if we choose to search our consciousness for it. Our soul incarnates with a particular learning objective. It would be impossible for our soul to accomplish its purpose if we retained our collective experiences. For this reason, our Spirit *chooses* what it will bring into each incarnation in terms of talents, predisposition, and natural skills.

In this life, my father brought into this experience much of the magician's power and knowledge. The magician had acquired his abilities through long and disciplined training in the mystery schools of the 16ᵗʰ century. My dad had these faculties naturally, without training or specialized study. He chose to use them for personal gratification rather than for spiritual understanding. Of course, it is possible that his soul's objective was to see what would happen if one had these powers and no discipline or spiritual direction. It is impossible to say for certain. What is certain is that he had his own soul's experience and played an important part in mine.

Regarding Forgiveness

What did you mean when you said the Monastery Child was able to forgive herself?

Since there is no gray-haired father figure sitting in judgment of humanity, the only one endowed with the ability to forgive is *ourselves*. Therefore, since the Child felt the need to be forgiven, the only one to do that was herself. When she and I connected and she realized there was no heavenly judge to condemn her, she was able to release her feelings of guilt and experience Love.

What did you mean when you said true forgiveness is freedom?

We are never free as long as we are unaware of our spiritual nature. We can never be our *Self*. We can only be what we *imagine* ourselves to be. For example, we think of ourselves as children, parents, good person/bad person. With spiritual awareness, we recognize we were Life before birth. Therefore, we are not children so much as charges, not parents so much as guardians. We are neither good nor bad because we are Spirit Being

139

endowed with the qualities of Spirit. With this understanding, we can recognize that the events in our lifetime are the result of our Spirit seeking to experience *Itself.* It may *choose* to experience *Itself* as a victim, a heroine, a president, or a prisoner. But always, no matter what role It is playing, It is infinite, eternal spirit. It is our True Self.

True forgiveness is the recognition that *you and all others are infinite Spirit Being* having a finite human experience *with mutual consent.* When you acknowledge that *no one* or *no thing* can act or react to you without the consent of divine Self, you will recognize true forgiveness. *This is not forgiveness at all but is the FREEDOM to allow each Divine experience in your life to express itself at the level of your awareness.*

Regarding Healing

When you wrote that your revelations were healing, how did that work?

Healing means being restored to health or to a condition of wholeness. Each revelation and experience I had uncovered a layer of spiritual awareness that was buried under the rubble of misconceptions. These misconceptions were like debris covering pieces of a jigsaw puzzle and as the debris began to shift, I saw the pieces clearly and began to discern how and where they fit in the wholeness of Spirit. Since part of the soul's journey is returning to the awareness that we *are* whole, the more Truth that is revealed, the closer we get to that conscious state of *Oneness,* the Whole Self.

You mentioned several times that your soul needed to be healed. How can that be? Isn't it perfect already?

Yes, a soul is, was, and always will be perfect, but in order for the soul to have the desired experience in each lifetime, it must choose to forget its infinite nature. So you might say that we take on spiritual amnesia until we become conscious that we are Spirit Being. In this state of forgetfulness, we constantly give parts of ourselves away and deny other parts. This fragments the soul's energy. This is not a permanent state, nor does fragmentation mean separation so much as a spinning out and away from our core. Before Wholeness can be expressed, these fragments must be reeled in and assimilated back into the soul. This gathering process is what I meant by my soul needing to be healed.

What do you mean by "giving parts of ourselves away" and "denying parts of self"?

This is basic human behavior. As human beings, we have forgotten our Divine nature. We believe we have to either add or subtract something from ourselves in order to be whole. When we are *not* conscious of our spiritual roots, we may give up parts of ourselves in order to gain love and/or recognition, as did the French woman, and/or approval of other people, as did the Crusader. Every time we act in a way that goes against what we feel to be true, we spin off a piece of our soul. Acting out of obligation, seeing ourselves as a victim, or accepting other people's limitations as our own without exploring our own strengths are common ways to fragment ourselves.

Every time we deny a part of ourselves, we spin off a piece of our soul. Each of us has parts of our psyche that we would like to deny exist. But the truth is, as humans we have a full spectrum of emotions and thoughts in our bank of experiences. This is as Spirit designed it. We may choose not to expand or explore some of these avenues, but if we wish to be whole, we must claim them. If we have a temper, we may not want to let it run rampant. Yet we must remember it is a part of the soul energy we brought in to work with. In the eyes of our soul, our temper is neither good nor bad. It is just energy the soul wishes to explore. If we deny we have it, we are in essence denying a part of our Spirit.

We are like a rare a coin. It takes both sides, heads and tails, to make it valuable. You cannot cut off one side because you don't like the way it looks and still have a whole coin.

Miscellaneous

How does your concept of "many Gods" differ from the Ancients who worshipped many gods?

Ancient cultures worshipped gods as things or idols—anything other than the divine Self within. This is having other gods before God. What I discerned was Creator Beings expressing *as* Their creation.

Do you walk around thinking you're God?

I walk around remembering that we are *all* God, regardless of appearances. We are all the offspring of the Divine Creative Principle and made of Divine Creative Substance. Since that Substance and what created the Substance are one and the same, we are all God, appearing as individual "you" and individual "me."

What's the difference between the ego, or personal self, and Spirit Self?

The ego self is the restricted view of ourselves that includes our body, our personality traits, our perceptions of me, my, mine, our opinions, and our judgments. It subtly or overtly believes that we did not exist before birth and will cease to exist at death. It is the part of us that sees itself as existing separate from everyone and everything outside itself.

The Spirit Self is the GOD Self. It is the part of us that *is* our Life. It is invisible, eternal, All-Knowing, and Infinite. It is our only True Identity. It recognizes and rejoices in the Oneness of all existence.

The ego is what allows us to have a *human* experience. It is the *vehicle* for our journey—not the journey itself. If the ego does not remember that it exists *only* because Spirit gives it life, it begins to think it is in charge. It makes decisions and judgments based on what it experiences through the physical senses and the intellect. Such limited perception does not encourage growth of our true potential. It is a shallow, isolated, and unfulfilling existence.

When the personal self or ego becomes aware of its bond with Spirit and consents to Spirit's higher guidance, life makes sense and becomes meaningful. We then live in harmony, cooperation, and reverence. We bring heaven to Earth.

What is the difference between inspiration and what you have described as your experiences?

I see inspiration as an inner prompting or a *new* idea. It is not complete in and of itself. As an idea, it has no substance or permanence and some action must give it form. If no action is taken, the idea will remain forever an inspiration. The experiences related in this book were actual happenings with a concreteness about them that *did* change my life in a permanent way without me taking direct action. Had they been only inspiration, it would have taken years of constant discipline and conscious commitment for my beliefs to change.

How can I or anyone else have the kind of experiences you've had?

We each have our own Truth established within us. That Truth will express itself in a way that you can understand and use. It will be individual to you. Your experiences can be very powerful yet certainly different from mine. Do not have an expectation as to *how* your spirit will tap on the door of your consciousness. What you can *do* is live as consciously as possible and create a space for quiet and reverence in your life.

Equally important is giving yourself permission to experience. Do not be afraid to allow yourself to step into the unknown, to hear, feel, and see nonphysical things for which you have no frame of reference. If you allow yourself such experiences and they are true and gifted encounters, they will manifest Truth in your life. Remember that any truth revealed is for *practical* incorporation into your life. So if you're having experiences in the "ozone" somewhere with no evidence of change toward a more harmonious life, then you may simply be having a mental trip. Only you can determine that, but if your sincere intention is for spiritual awakening and not for personal power and elitism, each experience will confirm itself.

Didn't it bother you that most of these experiences caused you to cry all the time?

Actually, no. At the time, the crying seemed a natural cleansing action.

Imagine you have a glass bottle with an extremely narrow neck. At first, the bottle is filled with pure water. Over time you add bits of dirt into the bottle. Slowly the water becomes dark and muddy. The dirt gets so impacted that even if you turn the bottle upside down, you can't get the dirty water to flow out. So you would flush the bottle with clear water until the dirt was washed out.

In this analogy, the bottle represents our present, future, and past lives, the pure water is our Divine Self, and the dirt is the erroneous beliefs and limitations that we accept as true. I see each of my experiences as Divine Self pouring Its energies into me. As this happened, it stirred up all the feelings, mis-truths, and false ideas I had carried around from lifetime to lifetime and flushed them out. Tears were my method of flushing the densest, most compact energies surrounding my misconceptions of Self and God. As time has progressed, those misconceptions have become more subtle and complex, as has my reaction to the influx of spiritual energy. Now I rarely cry with each new insight. Instead, my body registers a subtle energetic conversion. I imagine this, too, will change.

When you refer to your "true home" and Night Sky seeing his "home," are you saying you are some kind of ET or alien?

I am saying that being at one with my God is home. Perceiving myself operating outside of that Oneness is feeling alien.

Do you have any advice for those of us who are just becoming conscious of our spiritual journey?
My only advice is to *trust your own Truth and your intuition. Your Truth is your gift to life. Do not be afraid to BE that Truth.* I prefer not to give advice, but I'll offer a few things that have been helpful for me:

- Learn to meditate.
- Gain a solid foundation in one particular aspect of spiritual interpretation at a time, rather than skipping around studying different paths of awareness.
- Develop a support group of people who are interested in studying whatever path you are exploring at the time.
- Remain open to new experiences and New Age material, but at the same time don't be afraid to say, "No thanks. That is not my path."
- Get some bodywork such as network chiropractic, deep tissue massage, breath work, Huna Kane, and explore techniques such as "Twelve-Stage Healing" (Dr. Donald Epstein). These and other methods support the body as the nervous system becomes more refined and sensitive to spiritual input.
- Breathe. Breath is what integrates Spirit and body, making the spiritual energy usable in a practical way. What has helped me is to consciously force myself to breathe regular and full breaths when in meditation or spiritual communication. This serves two purposes. First, it keeps my mind from spinning off in some imagined direction, and second, it blends the incoming energy with my present state. Of course, in time this may change and becoming so still as not to breathe may more appropriate.
- Always trust your own inner guidance first.
- Keep a journal. Record whatever insights or experiences you receive in meditation or any spontaneous impart from your spirit.

SECTION IV

Everything in this book may be false.

EPILOGUE

Hopefully the insights in this book reveal that Truth is a living substance changing, maturing, and becoming the fullness of its innate self. The result of such a ripening process calls for an epilogue. I have written about my past lives, knowing them to be true and gifted memories of the continuing identity that I am. Now I must reveal that there is no such thing as a past life, nor can there be RE-incarnation. Before you throw your hands up in despair, let me explain.

Can you agree that time, as we perceive it, does not exist? We think in terms of linear time (past, present, and future) because that allows us a certain kind of experience, but the reality is that the only time that can exist is *NOW*. The past is beyond our reach and the future never arrives. So from the linear perspective, there is only *NOW*.

But if there is only *NOW*, how was it possible for me to interact with the Child in the monastery? How was she able to speak to me and offer her gratitude for my intervention?

Imagine time not as a straight line going toward spiritual awakening, but as a circle, with no beginning and no ending.

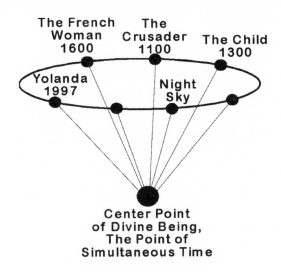

Our Divine Spirit Being has many experiences on this circle and must *focus Its awareness* in order to experience *Itself as* individual Being, as individual you and individual me.

I envision this as a circle with the various lifetimes situated around it, so no one life comes before or after another, or is more significant than another. The circle represents Divine Being's eternality. We perceive Divine Being expressing Its diversity as the various past, present, and future lives of our Divine Self.

In this illustration, the lifetimes on the circle unite in the center where all experiences become *one*. If you were at the Center Point, you would distinguish little separation between each sphere, or lifetime. As you moved away from the Center Point, you would notice a greater separation. At the Center Point, we live a more awakened existence. The further in consciousness we get from that point, the more forgetful we are of our True Self and the more we would identify with one particular lifetime.

This explains how the experiences related in this book were able to happen. The time-space doorway experience of the Monastery Child became clear. We both had moved toward the center point; she through her despair and me through meditation. We found ourselves in a moment of NOW time, able to interact and offer love and recognition to each other.

Can you see how the Child in the monastery and I could interact? Can you understand how I was able to feel and say that, "I had become one with the French Woman, the Crusader, and Night Sky? Does it seem possible that there can be no *past* life, no *re*incarnation. Our Divine Self is having these "lifetimes" simultaneously, and they all coexist in the center point.

When we move to the Center Point, everything is *available to us at that Now moment.* All the coexisting experiences that our Divine Being is having are accessible. We may influence our present life and interact with those other "lives." Our life and those "other lives" are all happening *NOW*, not in some distant past or future. Because it is all in the *NOW*, we can alter our "past" experiences as with the Child in the monastery. When I intervened in that "past life" (which was her present), it altered both our presents. It allowed the child to expand her perception of God and Self, saving her from personal judgment and suffering. It transformed my present by causing my perception to expand from "past lives" to *NOW* moments. I could discern that we do not RE-incarnate because we *are* incarnate *NOW*—no beginning and no ending, only an eternal *NOW*.

You might ask, "So what? How does this effect my life?" These experiences were all earlier in linear history but the same is true for the future. When we connect at the Center Point, everything that "future" Selves learn and experience is also available to us. Our present life can be influenced by reaching the Center Point and meeting All. At that moment, we may accept into our present experience the awareness of our future selves (in linear terms). This is what the Child in the monastery did. It was how she was able to mature in Consciousness and come to thank me.

Future (in linear terms) does not necessarily mean more evolved. The Crusader and Night Sky existed earlier in history, yet were more evolved in some ways then me, and I have learned a great deal from them.

Time is far different from what we may believe. When Night Sky saw his "home," he really saw his future self. He had been walking the future of the continent and somehow slipped into his own future and witnessed his own emergent God-Being. It was a vision of such vastness that he could only comprehend it as something separate from himself.

I hope that if this epilogue resonates as true, you will not mind its brevity. There is so much more to contemplate and each day brings a more refined appreciation for "NOW TIME."

I have flashes of standing in the Center Point and seeing its multidimensional patterning. I have tried to explain the blueprint with words and diagrams but I ask myself, "Can Infinity be described in language? Can eternity be illustrated?"

My intent in writing this book was to illustrate, through my experiences, that a person does not have to die to understand and experience eternal Life. That doesn't seem quite so important now.

It doesn't matter whether you believe what you have read in these pages, or even agree with it. What does matter is your *own* gift of Consciousness. Can you remember *WHO* you are? *WHERE* you come from? *WHAT* your true nature is?

About the Author

Yolanda Zigarmi Martin has been actively involved with spiritual work for the past eighteen years, teaching and lecturing. She lives in Atlanta, Georgia with her husband and their two cats, Alexander and Anastasia. When in Atlanta, she enjoys working in her garden, painting, and cooking.

Ms. Martin recognizes that Gifts may generate questions from readers and welcomes letters to the following address:

Gifts,
PO Box 28917,
Atlanta, GA 30328

Ms. Martin is available for lectures and workshops, and may be contacted at (404) 893-9170.

You can also visit her E-mail and Internet web site at:
www.netcom.com/~yzmartin

About the Publisher and Logo

The name "Oughten" was revealed to the publisher fourteen years ago, after three weeks of meditation and contemplation. The combined effect of the letters carries a vibratory signature, signifying humanity's ascension on a planetary level.

The logo represents a new world rising from its former condition. The planet ascends from the darker to the lighter. Our experience of a dark and mysterious universe becomes transmuted by our planet's rising consciousness — glorious and spiritual. The grace of God transmutes the dross of the past into gold, as we leave all behind and ascend into the millennium.

Our imprint includes books in a variety of fields and disciplines which emphasize our relationship to the rising planetary consciousness. Literature which relates to the ascension process, personal growth, and our relationship to extraterrestrials is our primary focus. We are also developing a line of beautifully illustrated children's books, which deal with all aspects of spirituality. The list that follows is only a sample of our current offerings. To obtain a complete catalog, contact us at the address shown at the back of this book.

Publisher's Comment

Our mission and purpose is to publish ascension books and complementary material for all peoples and all children worldwide. We urge you to share the information with your friends, and to join our network of spiritually-oriented people.

We currently serve over fifty authors, musicians, and artists. They need your support to get their messages to all nations. Our financial proceeds are recycled into producing new ascension books and expanding our distribution worldwide. If you have been financially blessed by the universe and would like to support this important endeavor, we ask you to consider becoming an investor in Oughten House. Please contact us.

Books on Ascension

An Ascension Handbook, by Tony Stubbs. A practical presentation which describes the ascension process in detail and includes several exercises to help you integrate it into your daily life. With humor and warmth, it brings ascension to "where we live," treading lightly but firmly over such topics as love, power, and truth; energy and matter; breaking old patterns; aligning with Spirit; and life as a Lightworker.
  – *ISBN 1-880666-08-1, $12.95*

Bridge Into Light: Your Connection to Spiritual Guidance, by Pam and Fred Cameron. Lovingly offers many step-by-step exercises on how to meditate and how to connect with your own inner guidance and guides. Also gives simple and clear ways to invoke the protection and assistance of the Masters. (Companion tape available.)
  – *ISBN 1-880666-07-3, $11.95*

What Is Lightbody? Archangel Ariel, channeled by Tashira Tachiren. Offers a twelve-level model for the ascension process, leading to the attainment of our Light Body. Recommended in *An Ascension Handbook*, this book gives many invocations, procedures, and potions to assist us on our journey home. Related tapes available.
  – *ISBN 1-880666-25-1, $12.95*

Heart Initiation, by Julienne Everett. Speaks to the seeker on the path who wants to know how to become totally free and why love is so important to freedom, whether ascension has to be difficult and painful, or whether there is an easier way, and what are the challenges and rewards of conscious ascension.
  ISBN 1-880666-36-7, $14.95

My Ascension Journal by Nicole Christine. Transform yourself and your life by using the journalizing methods given in this book. Includes several real-life examples from the author's own journals, plus many blank pages on which to write your own ascension story. This quality bound edition will become a treasured keepsake to be re-read over and over again.
  – *ISBN 1-880666-18-9, $11.95*

Cosmic Tales

The Corporate Mule: Don't Give Up Your Soul for the Company Goal, by Robert V. Gerard. In this "slice-of-life" novel, follow Scott, an idealistic graduate, into the real world of corporate politics...and a very rude awakening! Will he "crash and burn in corporate hell" or will he pull out of his self-destructive nose-dive in time?
– _ISBN 1-880666-04-9, $14.95_

Lady From Atlantis, by Robert V. Gerard. Shar Dae, the future empress of Atlantis, is suddenly transported onto a rain-soaked beach in modern America. There she meets her twin flame and discovers her mission: to warn the people of planet Earth to mend their ways before Mother Earth takes matters in her own hands!
– _ISBN 1-880666-21-9, $12.95_

Voice in the Mirror: Will The Final Apocalypse Be Averted? by Lee Shargel. In this first novel of The Chulosian Chronicles, Lee skilfully weaves fact and fiction to tell a thrilling story of extraterrestrials using the Hubble telescope to warn of impending planetary disaster. But can we overcome greed and fear to avert disaster? And that's only the beginning...
– _ISBN 1-880666-54-5, $23.95._

Cosmic Wisdom

The Extraterrestrial Vision by Gina Lake. Through Gina, Theodore, a nonphysical entity, tells us what we need to know about our extraterrestrial heritage and how to prepare for direct contact with those species of ET that will soon be appearing in our midst.
– _ISBN 1-880666-19-7, $13.95_

ET Contact: Blueprint for a New World by Gina Lake. Through Gina, the Confederation of Planets tells us what life on Earth will be like following mass contact with extraterrestrials, and what we must do to prepare in terms of changing institutions such as education, religion, politics, economics, the media, and most important, how we personally must change.
– _ISBN 1-880666-62-6, $12.95_

The Angels of the Rays by Johanna. A set of twelve lavish, full color Angel pictures with supporting descriptions and invocations. Includes a push-out color card for each Angel. *Makes a stunning gift!*
— *ISBN 1-880666-34-0, $19.95. (Additional card sets $12.95)*

Self-Help &Transformational Tools

Intuition by Design, by Victor R. Beasley, Ph.D. A boxed set of 36 IQ (Intuition Quotient) Cards contain consciousness-changing geometry on one side and transformational verse on the other. The companion book tells you the many ways to use the cards in all aspects of your life. An incredible gift to yourself and someone you love. Highly recommended for bringing your life into alignment with the Higher Mind of Source.
— *ISBN 1-880666-22-7, $21.95*

Navigating the 90s by Deborah Soucek. Practical ways to deal with today's chaotic times, and claim your soverignty when others would trample it. Focuses on ways of freeing ourselves from our past conditioning and imprinting, and provides simple, yet overlooked advice in reclaiming our true selves. Packed with pertinent observations and useful exercises.
— *ISBN 1-880666-47-2, $13.95*

Design Your Intention: An Experience in Embodying Source, by Ruth Ford-Crenshaw. Join Ruth as she relives the "spiritual highs" of her path, and through her, meet such movers and shakers of the metaphysical world as Chris Griscom, Drunvalo, and Tashira Tachiren. Contains many invaluable excerpts from the spiritual classics.
— *ISBN 1-880666-63-4, $12.95*

Love and Hope: A Message for the New Millenium, by Kiyo Sasaki Monro. A delightfully written book of wisdom that the author has gleaned on her path, with autobiographical notes, and an extensive question-and-answer section derived from live presentations. An ideal "starter book" for someone new to metaphysics or as a thoughtful gift for a friend.
— *ISBN 1-880666-56-1, $14.95*

OUGHTEN HOUSE FOUNDATION, INC.

The ascension process presents itself as a new reality for many of us on planet Earth. Many Starseeds and Lightworkers seek to know more. Thousands of people worldwide are reaching out to find others of like mind and to network with them. Oughten House Foundation stands ready to serve you all.

Oughten House Foundation, Inc. is a educational and networking organization whose purpose is to serve those seeking personal, social, and spiritual empowerment. Virtually all authors and affiliate authors of Oughten House Publications have developed and delivered high caliber seminars and workshops on their materials. Their works, sponsored by the Foundation, are internationally respected and in demand.

The Foundation holds a non-profit status and seeks members and affiliated Light Centers. If you or your center would like more information, please call 510-447-2332.

We will do our best to keep you and your network of friends up to date with ascension-related literature, materials, author tours, workshops, and channeling. And if you have a network database or small mailing list you would like to share, please send it along.

CATALOG REQUESTS & BOOK ORDERS

We will gladly send you a catalog on request. Simply call the *toll-free* number below, send in the Business Reply Card at the back of the book, or visit our on-line Internet bookstore at the web site below.

Book orders must be prepaid: check, money order, international coupon, VISA, MasterCard, Discover Card, and American Express accepted.

To place your order, call, fax, or mail to:

OUGHTEN HOUSE PUBLICATIONS

PO Box 2008
Livermore · California · 94551-2008 · USA
Phone: (510) 447-2332
Toll-free: 1- (888) ORDER IT
Fax: (510) 447-2376
E-mail: oughtenhouse.com
Internet: www.oughtenhouse.com